Social Urbanism and the Politics of Violence

DOI: 10.1057/9781137397362.0001

Other Palgrave Pivot titles

Eileen Piggot-Irvine: **Goal Pursuit in Education Using Focused Action Research**

Serenella Massidda: **Audiovisual Translation in the Digital Age: The Italian Fansubbing Phenomenon**

John Board, Alfonso Dufour, Yusuf Hartavi, Charles Sutcliffe and Stephen Wells: **Risk and Trading on London's Alternative Investment Market: The Stock Market for Smaller and Growing Companies**

Franklin G. Mixon, Jr: **Public Choice Economics and the Salem Witchcraft Hysteria**

Elisa Menicucci: **Fair Value Accounting: Key Issues Arising from the Financial Crisis**

Nicoletta Pireddu: **The Works of Claudio Magris: Temporary Homes, Mobile Identities, European Borders**

Larry Patriquin: **Economic Equality and Direct Democracy in Ancient Athens**

Antoine Pécoud: **Depoliticising Migration: Global Governance and International Migration Narratives**

Gerri Kimber: **Katherine Mansfield and the Art of the Short Story: A Literary Modernist**

C. Paul Hallwood and Thomas J. Miceli: **Maritime Piracy and Its Control: An Economic Analysis**

Letizia Guglielmo and Lynée Lewis Gaillet (editors): **Contingent Faculty Publishing in Community: Case Studies for Successful Collaborations**

Katie Digan: **Places of Memory: The Case of the House of the Wannsee Conference**

Mario La Torre: **The Economics of the Audiovisual Industry: Financing TV, Film and Web**

Piero Formica: **The Role of Creative Ignorance: Portraits of Path Finders and Path Creators**

James Carson: **The Columbian Covenant: Race and the Writing of American History**

Tomasz Kamusella: **Creating Languages in Central Europe During the Last Millennium**

Imad A. Moosa and Kelly Burns: **Demystifying the Meese–Rogoff Puzzle**

Kazuhiko Togo and GVC Naidu (editors): **Building Confidence in East Asia: Maritime Conflicts, Interdependence and Asian Identity Thinking**

Aylish Wood: **Software, Animation and the Moving Image: What's in the Box?**

Mo Jongryn (editor): **MIKTA, Middle Powers, and New Dynamics of Global Governance: The G20's Evolving Agenda**

Holly Jarman: **The Politics of Trade and Tobacco Control**

Cruz Medina: **Reclaiming Poch@ Pop: Examining the Rhetoric of Cultural Deficiency**

David McCann: **From Protest to Pragmatism: The Unionist Government and North-South Relations from 1959–72**

Thijl Sunier and Nico Landman: **Transnational Turkish Islam: Shifting Geographies of Religious Activism and Community Building in Turkey and Europe**

Daria J. Kuss and Mark D. Griffiths: **Internet Addiction in Psychotherapy**

Elisa Giacosa: **Innovation in Luxury Fashion Family Business: Processes and Products Innovation as a Means of Growth**

DOI: 10.1057/9781137397362.0001

palgrave▸pivot

Social Urbanism and the Politics of Violence: The Medellín Miracle

Kate Maclean

*Lecturer in Social Geography, Birkbeck,
University of London, UK*

palgrave
macmillan

DOI: 10.1057/9781137397362.0001

First published 2015 by
PALGRAVE MACMILLAN

Palgrave Macmillan in the UK is an imprint of Macmillan Publishers Limited, registered in England, company number 785998, of Houndmills, Basingstoke, Hampshire, RG21 6XS.

Palgrave Macmillan in the US is a division of St Martin's Press LLC, 175 Fifth Avenue, New York, NY 10010.

Palgrave Macmillan is the global academic imprint of the above companies and has companies and representatives throughout the world.

Palgrave® and Macmillan® are registered trademarks in the United States, the United Kingdom, Europe and other countries.

ISBN: 978–1–137–39737–9 EPUB
ISBN: 978–1–137–39736–2 PDF
ISBN: 978–1–137–39735–5 Hardback

This book is printed on paper suitable for recycling and made from fully managed and sustained forest sources. Logging, pulping and manufacturing processes are expected to conform to the environmental regulations of the country of origin.

A catalogue record for this book is available from the British Library.

A catalog record for this book is available from the Library of Congress.

www.palgrave.com/pivot

DOI: 10.1057/9781137397362

Contents

List of Figures

DOI: 10.1057/9781137397362.0002

Acknowledgements

Many, many thanks are due to all those who gave their support, both in Colombia and in the United Kingdom, during the development of this project. First, I am eternally grateful to all the participants in this research for giving so generously of their time. I would also like to acknowledge the support of staff at the Sub-Secretariat for Women in Medellín, and in particular Liliana Escobar, Luz Nely Osorno, Isabel Agudelo, and Marta Celia Hoyos, for allowing me insight into the truly amazing work that they do; the members of the Comité Intergremial de Antioquia, especially Carlos Mario Echeverri, for the warm welcome they extended to me on each of my visits to their city; Mario Enrique Vargas and Carlos Andrés Jiménez of the Escuela de Administración, Finanzas y Tecnología [School of Administration, Finance and Technology – EAFIT] for organising the seminar 'Rompiendo el Cristal' ['Breaking the Glass Ceiling'] at which I spoke in October 2011, and for showing me the work of EAFIT Social; Milford Bateman for first introducing me to Medellín and for our work together on numerous subsequent projects; Jonathan Glennie at the Overseas Development Institute for his insights and support on fieldwork; and Enrique Castañon Ballivián for providing excellent interview transcriptions as well as assistance throughout the research process.

In the United Kingdom, I would like to extend thanks to all at the Developmental Leadership Program (DLP), whose generous funding made this research possible, and in particular deepest gratitude goes to the late Adrian Leftwich, the DLP's founding Director of Research, whose experience, expertise, and enthusiasm run throughout this project. Also at the DLP, David Hudson of University College London generously gave insights and detailed feedback, and Heather Lyne de Ver was a fount of patience and administrative support. My publisher at Palgrave Macmillan – Christina Brian – has been encouraging and extremely efficient from the outset. I would also like to thank colleagues in the Geography, Environment and Development Department at Birkbeck for providing such a constructive working atmosphere – not to mention all the cakes. Finally, I would like to thank my friends and family for their support, patience, and comments on this book, and in particular my mum and dad, not only for their unfailing confidence in me, but also for all those lively political discussions about Thomas Hobbes.

DOI: 10.1057/9781137397362.0003

List of Abbreviations

AUC	Autodefensas Unidas de Colombia [United Self-Defence Forces of Colombia]
BCN	Bloque Cacique Nutibara [Cacique Nutibara Block, a paramilitary group]
BRIC countries	Brazil, Russia, India, China
CEDEZOs	Centros de Desarrollo Empresarial Zonal [Zonal Business Development Centres]
CJA	Centre for Justice and Accountability
COOSERCOM	Cooperativa de Vigilancia y Servicio a la Comunidad [Cooperative Surveillance and Community Service]
EAFIT	Escuela de Administración, Finanzas y Tecnología [School of Administration, Finance and Technology]
ELN	Ejército de Liberación Nacional [National Liberation Army]
EPM	Empresas Publicas de Medellín [Public Companies of Medellín]
FARC	Fuerzas Armadas Revolucionarias de Colombia [Revolutionary Armed Forces of Colombia]
GEA	Grupo Empresarial Antioqueño [Antioquian Business Group]
HDI	Human Development Index
IPC	Instituto Popular de Capacitación [Popular Capacitation Institute]

M19	Movimiento 19 de Abril [Movement of the 19th of April]
NGO	non-governmental organisation
PePEs	Perseguidos por Pablo Escobar [People Persecuted by Pablo Escobar]
PMIB	Programa de Mejoramiento Integral de Barrios [Integral Slum Improvement Programme]
PRIMED	Programa Integral de Mejoramiento de Barrios Subnormales [Integral Programme for the Improvement of Informal Settlements in Medellín]
PUI	Proyecto Urbano Integral [Integrated Urban Upgrading Project]
UNDP	United Nations Development Programme
UNODC	United Nations Office on Drugs and Crime
URBAM	Centro de Estudios Urbanos y Ambientales [Centre for Urban and Environmental Studies]
VPA	Violence Prevention Alliance
WHO	World Health Organization

DOI: 10.1057/9781137397362.0004

Introduction: The Medellín Miracle

Abstract: *Medellín, Colombia, was once the most violent city on Earth. In recent years, however, the city has gained prominence not for its association with narco-traffic and the notorious Pablo Escobar, but for the regeneration policies, known as 'social urbanism', which appear to have dramatically reduced the city's violence. Social urbanism was designed to address violence by tackling inequality and exclusion in the city, with projects including innovative public transport networks, public parks, and libraries. Although social urbanism has globally been deemed a miraculous success, within Medellín many are concerned that these developments are becoming too oriented towards city branding. In this polemic context, this volume identifies the political negotiations, coalitions, and compromises that took place behind the miracle, and the complexity and significance of the political processes involved.*

Keywords: city branding; social urbanism; urban violence

Maclean, Kate. *Social Urbanism and the Politics of Violence: The Medellín Miracle*. Basingstoke: Palgrave Macmillan, 2015. DOI: 10.1057/9781137397362.0005.

Medellín, the capital of the Department of Antioquia, Colombia, was once the most murderous city on Earth. In the 1980s and 1990s, the city became known as the epicentre of the global trade in cocaine, and notorious drug lord Pablo Escobar and his Medellín Cartel were seen as largely responsible for the astonishing increase in violence at this time. At the peak of the violence in 1991, there were 375 homicides per 100,000 population in Medellín (Uran, 2010: 129). This figure was more than 35 times the World Health Organization's definition of epidemic violence, which is 10 per 100,000 (UNDP 2013), and even compared unfavourably with the Colombian average for that year, which was 79 (Figure 1). In addition to the extreme levels of violence perpetrated and orchestrated by the cartel, violence involving paramilitaries, urban militia, and, indeed, the State was endemic in Medellín, creating a situation in which violence became 'banal' (Pécaut, 1999).

It would appear, however, that Medellín's darkest days have passed, and the city is now known for the astonishing decline in violence that has occurred over the last 20 years. Although the statistics show that

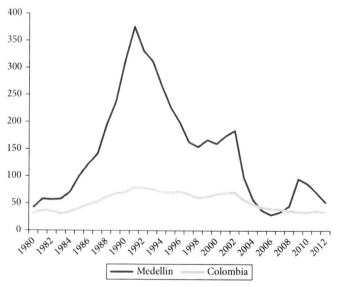

FIGURE 1   *Homicide rate per 100,000 population in Medellín and Colombia, 1980–2012*

Sources: Uran, 2010: 129; Medellín Como Vamos, http://www.Medellíncomovamos. org/seguridad-y-convivencia; UNODC, http://data.un.org/Data. aspx?d=UNODC&f=tableCode%3A1

DOI: 10.1057/9781137397362.0005

Medellín still has some way to go, they are now comparable to those for major cities in the United States, and the murder rate in Medellín for 2013 was 39 per 100,000 (Medellín Como Vamos, n.d.). This sharp decline, known as the 'Medellín Miracle', has become associated with the approach to urban development pioneered in the city known as 'social urbanism'. 'Social urbanism' is an umbrella term for the policies enacted in Medellín during the late 1990s and early 2000s. Two discourses have framed the development of social urbanism since the 1990s. The first is the idea that there is a 'historical social debt' owed by the elites of the city to the poorer, marginalised areas on the hillsides that have been neglected and excluded in the city's development and planning. The second is a recognition of the need to 'change the skin of the city', to address the spatial exclusion that had underpinned the rise to power of various violent actors (Echeverri & Orsini, 2012). This is a particularly urban focus on the problem of violence, which, in its diagnosis, formulation, and execution, espouses the idea not only that inequality and exclusion underpin violence but also that violence is framed by the city's political geography – the way that power is constructed, gained, and maintained in different areas.

Investments in infrastructure, public transport, and conspicuous architectural projects in the poorest neighbourhoods of the city were designed to address the inequitable development of the past that had led to the outskirts of the city becoming neglected, excluded, and violent. This approach won Medellín the Urban Land Institute's award for Innovative City of the Year, 2013, sponsored by Citibank and the *Wall Street Journal*. However, despite these successes, many fear that the focus has increasingly centred on changing the city's image rather than the deep-rooted political causes of the unrest, and that many of the policies associated with social urbanism reaffirm as much as challenge elite power and dominance. There is great concern that the implementation of these policies was preceded by a 'pacification' of crime-ridden areas by the State military, allegedly with the collusion of paramilitary groups, that resulted, according to international human rights agencies, in a high number of civilian casualties.

It is clear that the murder rate alone, whilst clearly indicative of the city's problems with conflict, does not fully capture all the dimensions of the insecurity experienced in the city. The rate of kidnapping – vastly under-reported – reached extremely high levels in the 1980s and 1990s, and kidnapping was part of a landscape of bribery, extortion, and protection rackets that took hold in the city (Pécaut, 1999). Violent assault rates in some areas continue to be extremely high, as are the rates of gender-based violence, much of which takes place within the home, and for which statistics based on reporting are notoriously unreliable. Colombia's long-running conflict involving guerrilla, paramilitary, and militia armed groups, as well as State forces, frames Medellín's violence. However, as is clear in Figure 1, Medellín's violence far outweighed the Colombian national average, and it was thus more than a microcosm of the broader national conflict. It is also important to remember that given the vast inequality in Medellín, statistics at the city scale may oversimplify. Whilst the homicide rate in 2013 was 39 per 100,000 for Medellín as a whole, the rate in one of the poorer neighbourhoods, La Candelaria, was 165 (Medellín Como Vamos, n.d.).

Medellín is a paradigmatic example of 'urban violence', a subject that gained prominence in late twentieth-century debates on security, as it was realised that not only does peacetime violence mostly occur in cities, but urban violence exceeds that found in wars (Muggah, 2013). Urban violence is correlated with rapid city growth and high levels of inequality, which combine to create particularly segregated urban spaces. High levels of urban violence are more likely to be found in countries, such as South Africa and Colombia, going through a transition to democracy from a period of long-term civil conflict. Medellín exemplifies these patterns. As Colombia's industrial heartland, it is a magnet for migration from surrounding rural areas. It is also the destination for many fleeing the ongoing civil conflict in Colombia, which is the country with the highest rates of internal displacement in the world (Carrillo, 2009). Medellín is regarded as one of the most unequal cities in Latin America, with Gini coefficients that frequently outrank even those of other large Colombian cities. As one former secretary of the mayoralty put it, differences within the city are such that 'it's like governing Switzerland and Bangladesh'.[1]

The political landscape in Medellín is highly unequal, exclusionary, and fraught. The exclusive neighbourhood of El Poblado, to the south of the city, boasts luxury hotels, shopping malls, and private universities that could rival those of cities in the 'developed' world. However, the areas to the northeast and northwest of the city, situated on the steep Andean mountain slopes, which are the areas where migrants to the city often arrive, are dominated by informal settlements, lack of infrastructure, high levels of poverty and indigency, and violent crime. It was in

DOI: 10.1057/9781137397362.0005

these areas, excluded after years of neglect by factional city elites who showed little interest in extending development to the city's new arrivals, that the various armed protagonists in Medellín's multiple 'theatres of violence' (Pécaut, 1999) gained power. The Medellín Cartel was able to offer riches and hopes of upward mobility that were otherwise denied to the city's excluded youth; the leftist militia, related to prominent Marxist guerrilla groups in rural areas, could offer security and a political identity in an increasingly violent context; and paramilitary groups in turn could offer to protect property and deal with growing rates of delinquency through 'cleaning' operations (Taussig, 2005). Formal State politicians, the judiciary, and the police, all of whom lacked legitimacy in these areas, were not only incapable of suppressing this rise in violence but also complicit or allegedly in collusion with the city's armed groups (Carroll, 2011; Tubb, 2013).

As a city that exhibits the textbook characteristics of urban violence, developments in Medellín are instructive in critiquing the theories which frame the indicators of urban violence. The contention of this book, substantiated by an empirical exploration of the development of social urbanism, is that to understand urban violence, the significance of inequality and exclusion has to be placed in broader cultural, historical, and political context. The technical interventions that have come to define the miracle – the infrastructure projects, iconic architecture, and development of public spaces – hence need to be analysed in terms of their role in political processes in the city. Medellín is a place where violence has entered into the 'common sense' of how politics is conducted. The potential of the miracle is that the long-term political processes behind the development of social urbanism have disrupted, to some degree, the prominence of violence as a means to attain and maintain power.

This book examines the political processes behind the Medellín Miracle, in particular the political fora that enabled the diagnosis of the city's problems as being rooted in inequality and marginalisation, and the subsequent formulation of appropriate policies. When the violence in Medellín was recognised as a crisis in 1991, political spaces opened up in which community organisations and social movements had a seat at the table with the city's notoriously exclusive and protectionist elites. As a result of these political changes, a new political party, – Compromiso Ciudadano – was formed, and its leader, Sergio Fajardo, eventually took office as mayor in 2004. The changes in the political fabric of Medellín, and the transformations in terms of urban development policies, were

DOI: 10.1057/9781137397362.0005

far more complex than the term 'miracle' suggests and involved constitutional changes at the national level, pressure from global economic forces, participation by a range of grassroots organisations and social movements, and, crucially, in terms of being able to enact a new agenda, the collaboration of the city's business and political elites. The discursive, institutional, and political spaces which opened up in the wake of Medellín's crisis, and the broader national and global transformations which were under way at this time, may have begun to change the way that power was gained and exercised in Medellín, and so had a role in reducing the prominence of violence in power struggles in the city.

By focusing on the political processes behind the 'miracle', this book draws and builds on theoretical and policy-oriented discussions of urban violence, particularly those which have stressed that violence – in its many forms – needs to be understood as a developmental and political issue (Jabri, 1996; Moser & McIlwaine, 2004). Drawing on work in urban geography, development studies, and political science on violence in cities, this book aims to address the following questions:

▸ How can violence be understood politically, and as an issue of urban geography and development?
▸ What distinguishes social urbanism from other urban interventions in Colombia and worldwide?
▸ How was the political consensus necessary to enact social urbanism achieved, and what does this indicate about how power struggles that shape violence in Medellín have changed?
▸ How can understanding the political processes behind the Medellín Miracle help us understand epidemic urban violence and policies that can reduce it?

The empirical research for this book was conducted during a number of visits that I made to Medellín in 2011 and 2012, as part of two different research projects. These trips included an extended stay in July and August 2012. I first visited Medellín in February 2011 with the economist Milford Bateman. This was a brief, targeted visit to explore the city's business support centres, known as CEDEZOs (Centros de Desarrollo Empresarial Zonal [Zonal Business Development Centres]; Bateman et al., 2011). Visits were made to CEDEZO projects around the city, and business leaders and council members who were involved in their development and management were interviewed. We also attended and presented at various fora at the Escuela de Administración, Finanzas y Tecnología [School of Administration, Finance and Technology – EAFIT], met with the business groups Pro-Antioquia and the Comité Intergremial de Antioquia, and visited the most prominent architectural and structural features associated with the Medellín Miracle, including the 'Metrocable', a cable-car which connects excluded neighbourhoods with the centre of the city, the libraries, and the various parks. In October of the same year, I was invited by EAFIT and the Sub-Secretariat for Women to present at the conference 'Rompiendo el Cristal' ['Breaking the Glass Ceiling'], on women and the labour market. During this stay, I visited various projects run by the sub-secretariat and the university's development programme, EAFIT Social. These projects included educational programmes for community mothers, training for community associations bidding for public contracts, community crèches, and cooperative businesses. My visits to these programmes were mediated by those involved in their implementation, but they nevertheless afforded an understanding of the breadth of projects that fell under the rubric of what has become known as social urbanism.

Following these visits, I developed a project with the Developmental Leadership Programme to explore the specific role of elites, leaders, and coalitions in the Medellín Miracle (Maclean, 2014a). The fieldwork for this project was carried out in July and August 2012, and included 30 interviews and 7 focus groups with leaders from the city's political and business elites, social movements, and community organisations who were involved in the political changes instigated by the recognition that the violence was at crisis point in 1991. The fieldwork also included visits to programmes to support income generation, cooperatives, and various educational and cultural projects run by the mayoralty, universities, and businesses. Press coverage and documents from the 1990s and 2000s, during which time social urbanism was being developed and implemented, including reports generated by investigations into the violence at the local, national, and international levels, were also analysed.

This remainder of this book is divided into five chapters and a brief conclusion. Chapter 1 discusses how violence, and in particular urban violence, has been explored theoretically, and how these theorisations relate to policy. Although violence is often seen either as a psychological trait or as an outcome of a breakdown in social order, the argument in this chapter is that violence is inherently political. The causes of violence, whether they are structural, economic, or cultural, need to be understood in terms of processes via which power is gained and maintained.

DOI: 10.1057/9781137397362.0005

Chapter 2, 'Medellín: The Most Violent City in the World', examines how violence came to be such a prominent part of political as well as everyday life in Medellín. Medellín's rapid growth and high levels of inequality and exclusion are placed in the context of Colombia's ongoing conflict among various armed groups and, of course, the rise to power of the notorious Medellín Cartel. The exclusivity of the city's patrimonial elites, ferociously proud of their region, and their neglect of the development of the outer regions of the city are central to understanding the excluded spaces which armed groups were able to exploit. The aim of this chapter is to show, framed by the theoretical stance outlined in Chapter 1, that violence was a continuation of political process in Medellín, rather than a breakdown of social order.

Chapter 3 presents 'The Miracle'. It examines the policies associated with social urbanism in the context of international models of urban regeneration. The specific interventions carried out – mass transport systems, public spaces, and iconic buildings – bear the hallmarks of urban regeneration orthodoxy at the turn of the century. They were explicitly inspired by the Catalan model that regenerated Barcelona, but the contention of this analysis is that their significance and effects need to be understood in terms of the political changes that they represent and create. To this end, the following two chapters look at the processes behind the Medellín Miracle.

Chapter 4 considers the broader structural context within which Medellín's decline in violence occurred, including constitutional and electoral reforms in Colombia and changes in relations with the United States. The focus of this chapter is the interventions in Medellín that followed the recognition that the city's violence had reached crisis point. The establishment of the Consejería Presidencial para Medellín [Presidential Programme for Medellín] and the recognition that the city needed to modernise to compete in a globalised world led to the development of reports, seminars, and fora at which the city's elites took a seat at the table with radical non-governmental organisations (NGOs) and community groups to discuss the city's problems and potential solutions.

The final chapter, 'New Political Spaces', looks at the way the political changes in the city were used by political groups, including Compromiso Ciudadano, and how these processes have begun to change the politics that underpinned the astronomical levels of violence that the city had experienced.

DOI: 10.1057/9781137397362.0005

Note

1 Member of the Fajardo administration, interview, 24 July 2012. Interviews were conducted by the author and transcribed by Enrique Castañón Ballivián. The translation of quotations in this book is the author's own.

DOI: 10.1057/9781137397362.0005

1

The Politics of Violence and Urbanism

Abstract: *This chapter provides the theoretical framing for the discussion of violence and social urbanism in Medellín, drawing on work from geography, urban studies, political science, and regionally specific explorations of violence in Latin American cities. Theories of violence have tended to situate the problem either with the individual, in terms of criminal pathology, or with structural inequality. This chapter proposes a more dynamic analysis of violence as process, with a focus on how violence becomes a means to attain and retain power, and how violence enters into the 'common sense' of political and social life. This framework can offer an analysis of how places become violent, how violence relates to urban politics and geography, and, as may be the case in Medellín, how transformations in political processes may address the root causes of violence.*

Keywords: theories of violence; subjectivity; urban violence; gender-based violence

Maclean, Kate. *Social Urbanism and the Politics of Violence: The Medellín Miracle.* Basingstoke: Palgrave Macmillan, 2015. DOI: 10.1057/9781137397362.0006.

DOI: 10.1057/9781137397362.0006

This chapter explores the ways in which violence has been conceptualised and analysed, with particular reference to violence in an urban context. Violence is a vast subject that has been studied from a variety of perspectives. The purpose of this overview is to argue for an approach that analyses violence in terms of power, and to contextualise such an understanding within broader policy and academic debates on the subject. Violence tends to be seen, in popular representations and psychological analyses, as a trait of individuals, but a sociopolitical approach can explain how *places* can be deemed 'violent'. This is pertinent to the development of social urbanism in Medellín, as, despite the fact that violence is associated with particularly villainous characters there, the claim is that a city-wide approach to urban regeneration has led to a reduction in violence.

Violence is ubiquitous, complex, and messy. Myriad incidents in which harm has been intended or effected, whether in the name of discipline, defence, revenge, or national security, as well as owing to negligence, can be categorised as 'violent'. Efforts to neatly define violence and classify its varied manifestations, whilst helpful for analysis and policy, necessarily simplify the astonishing range of cultural, historical, psychological, economic, and political factors that are involved in any act of violence (Nordstrom and Robben, 1995). The focus here is urban violence. 'Urban violence', like many of the other classifications of violence, describes a cluster of incidents that are similar and different in myriad ways. Criminal violence, political oppression, gang violence, and gender violence can all be considered typical of the violence to be found in the city. Nevertheless, urban violence is a phenomenon that has generated interest from a range of scholars and development practitioners, as well as the military, who have sought reasons to explain why violent crime is so high in cities around the world and policy solutions to address what many are calling urban violence of epidemic proportion.

The Violence Prevention Alliance (VPA), a branch of the World Health Organization, defines violence as

> the intentional use of physical force or power, threatened or actual, against oneself, another person, or against a group or community, that either results in or has a high likelihood of resulting in injury, death, psychological harm, maldevelopment, or deprivation. (WHO, 2014)

The VPA further categorises violence in terms of whether it is self-directed, interpersonal, or collective, and these categories are in turn

DOI: 10.1057/9781137397362.0006

divided into social, political, and economic in the case of collective violence, and physical, sexual, and psychological in the case of interpersonal violence. This typology demonstrates the complexity of violence and the range of violent acts, whilst keeping sight of the intuitive definition of violence as the use of force to inflict harm. It has been used as the basis of work on violence in economic and epidemiological studies from the WHO, and in other analyses that situate violence as a sociopolitical concern (Moncada, 2013; Moser and McIlwaine, 2004). This definition is broadly used, but its focus on intent is controversial and represents the tendency to limit discussions of the causes of violence to the motives of the perpetrator, in terms of either psychological traits or deprivation.

Psychological approaches to violence tend to explore the relationships between aggression, arousal, cognition, learning, and the propensity to commit violent acts (e.g. DeWall et al., 2011; Mazur, 2013). Whilst there is a recognition in this body of work of the need to situate psychological explanations of violence in the context of interdisciplinary research on the subject, there is nevertheless a focus on quantitative, generalisable studies that are often carried out under laboratory conditions. Although academic work in this field is characterised by specific, limited knowledge claims, at a political level the focus on individual causes of violence in positivist science can undermine the pursuit of more contextualised understandings (Feldman, 1991). The image of the perpetrator of violence as 'psychotic', or as a testosterone-fuelled gang member whose cognitive processes dictate his harmful acts and lack of empathy, is powerful not only in popular culture, but also at policy level. Although the 2010 World Bank Report on *Violence in the City* espouses an interdisciplinary approach, it suggests that social factors such as the experience of abuse can increase the propensity of the victim to become a perpetrator of violence on the ground that 'there is strong evidence that this experience alters brain physiology' (World Bank, 2010: 25). Such a reductionist approach may weaken resolve to act on social issues associated with violence in favour of pathologising the individuals involved. It also coincides with political agendas that focus on incarceration and punishment rather than prevention.

Despite the prominence of an individualistic approach to violence, consistent associations have been found between poverty, inequality, city size, and city growth that would suggest that structural social and economic conditions contribute to a propensity among people in certain places to resort to violence (Elgar and Aitken, 2011; Pridemore, 2011). It seems that inequality is a greater predictor of an area being violent

DOI: 10.1057/9781137397362.0006

than poverty, although of course high levels of poverty and high levels of inequality are often related. Although larger cities tend to be more violent, the crucial factor is the rate of city growth, which, if high, is consistently associated with elevated levels of urban violence (Muggah and Savage, 2012). Whilst the evidence for these correlations is compelling, the causal mechanisms involved are debatable, and highly politicised. Although it is established that certain socioeconomic factors are involved in violence and should be a focus of prevention strategies, in the search to find generalisable consistencies, assumptions about causal mechanisms involved in these correlations may not reflect the specific political context of a given city and may reinforce fears perpetuated in the media about the potential for violence among excluded populations, further stigmatising those groups.

Coming from a focus on peace rather than violence, Galtung (1969) proposed the term 'structural violence' to capture the harm done by living in conditions of poverty and inequality. Contrary to the WHO definition, Galtung's starting point is that peace is the absence of violence, and therefore, for peace to be desirable, the definition of violence must capture 'when human beings are being influenced so that their actual somatic and mental realizations are below their potential realizations' (Galtung, 1969: 168). Such a broad, and perhaps counterintuitive, definition of violence entails that, to follow his examples, the death of someone from tuberculosis in a context in which remedies are available, or the uneven access to transport that permits the 'mobility of [only] a selected few' (Galtung, 1969: 169), be regarded as violence. The idea of 'structural violence' goes beyond the observation of patterns of violence or correlations to suggest that deprivation itself is an act of violence. 'Structural violence' also refers to social patterns in violence. As Galtung puts it, 'when one husband beats his wife there is a clear case of personal violence, but when one million husbands keep one million wives in ignorance there is structural violence' (Galtung, 1969: 171).

Structural factors associated with violence, such as inequality, exclusion, and deprivation, do not by themselves explain violence or negate the importance of social context in understanding violent acts. Collective violence, as explored by Tilly (2003), involves damage, at least two perpetrators, and coordination between those perpetrators. This coordination does not necessarily mean prior agreement or a chain of command; it may be a (possibly tacit) consensus that violence is the right course of action. Such a consensus relies on shared understandings about which

DOI: 10.1057/9781137397362.0006

situations require violent reactions and ideas of identity that indicate who is deserving of violence and whose side one should be on (Jabri, 1996; Tizro, 2013). These ideas are constantly recreated and renegotiated as people interact and are specific to local histories, economies, societies, and cultures. Examples used to illustrate this point range from ideas of masculinity, honour, and solidarity that can start a bar fight (Tilly, 2003) to the systematic, genocidal violence of colonialism and holocaust, which may be underpinned by ideas of which beings 'count' as human, which bodies represent evil and which civility, how to maintain control, and, most disturbingly, how to pass the time (Taussig, 1984).

Understanding the discursive context is hence a necessary component of analyses of violence, and entails an exploration of violence in private spaces, notably the home – the site where discursive constructions under-pinning and justifying violence are recreated. Different types of violence need to be seen as an 'interrelated continuum' (Moser, 2004: 6) rather than being, as tends to be the case, dissociated from political conflicts, seen as epiphenomena of a broader conflict, or even assumed to be private, individual matters (Pearce, 2006). Such an interpretive approach that emphasises the recreation of discourses that justify violence is in danger of being confounded with ideas of a 'culture of violence'. Allegations that cultures are somehow inherently violent are not only, according to Pécaut (1999), a 'lazy' analysis but can also recreate harmful colonial tropes and, in effect, offer merely a tautologous explanation that a place is violent because it is like that there. Nevertheless, it is important to ground analyses of violence in cultural context (Galtung, 1990; Munck, 2008). Cultural discourses, which can themselves be understood only in historical context, underpin the identity categories that frame analyses of social exclusion, and the discourses via which 'normal' behaviour is defined, transgression is recognised, and the justifications of violence are established (Nordstrom and Robben, 1995).

Studying the violent *subject* – not the agent in isolation, but rather the person who is interpreting, negotiating, and even trying to change her circumstances – affords a framework for understanding how violence is underpinned by structural context, as well as how that structural context positions people in terms of their propensity to violence – not only with regard to motive but also in terms of the discursive and material resources and power to commit violent acts (Jabri, 1996). As Jabri argues, unless you are a pacifist, there will be some moment at which you think violence is justified. The most obvious example is self-defence, but justifiable violence

DOI: 10.1057/9781137397362.0006

can include examples as divergent as 'just wars', the death penalty, and disciplining children. That moment at which violence is considered to be justified is mediated by discourse, culture, and status, as well as being a response to material and structural 'realities'. Crucially, understanding the violent subject means foregrounding the interpretation and internalisation of ideas of identity, trust, and worth that are culturally situated in local historical, social, political, and economic contexts.

This position is a challenge to understandings of violence as the absence of order and authority. If it is accepted that the life of man (*sic*) is 'nasty, brutish and short' – a view espoused not only by Thomas Hobbes and contract theorists but also by evolutionary psychologists – and that the *raison d'etre* of authority is to appease and contain this brutishness, then violence is the disruption of social order. If, on the other hand, it is accepted that violence itself is mediated by social rules, norms, and discourses and situated in an economic, political context, then violence is *part* of a social order (Jabri, 1996). Furthermore, violence may be a critical element in the maintenance of hierarchies, identities, and norms which themselves underpin violence. For violence to continue, it has to be in certain interests that it continue (Tilly, 2003), and hence violence itself has a role in perpetuating political processes, rather than being an absence of such processes or of 'order' (Jabri, 1996). It therefore follows that violence cannot be fully understood without an analysis of power.

Violence and power

Discussions of violence and power have ranged from the global scale of inter-State nuclear war to so-called intimate partner violence. Violence and power have been understood to relate in various ways. Whilst Mao Zedong famously claimed that 'political power grows out of the barrel of a gun', Hannah Arendt argued that violence is the opposite of power, 'where the one rules absolutely, the other is absent' (Arendt, 1970: 56). Arendt's conceptual division involves a definition of power as consensus, which violence is incapable of creating. What violence can achieve in the immediate is 'effective command', and although violence appears when 'power is in jeopardy ... left to its own course it ends in power's disappearance' (Arendt, 1970: 56), as it erodes the consensual bases of legitimate power.

Arendt's configuration is a challenge to the conception of State power that has obtained for centuries in the liberal tradition, in which the State

DOI: 10.1057/9781137397362.0006

gains legitimacy by using force, in Hobbesian terms, to secure the security of its citizens, and hence can gain the consent – albeit tacit – of its citizens to obey its laws: the social contract. The need for a State that, as Weber argues, has a 'monopoly of the legitimate use of physical force within a given territory' (cited in Campbell and Dillon, 1993: 141) and is capable of suppressing the natural nasty brutishness of its citizens associates power and violence constitutively. The powerful heuristic device of the social contract has dominated vernacular understandings of violence as a breakdown in social order and justifies the repression of violence and disorder by forceful means.

The understanding of violence as a breakdown in the social contract provides an analytical framework capable of explaining the relationship between inequality, deprivation, and violence as a failure of power to secure citizens' security, broadly defined. If for whatever reason the State fails to be the sole wielder of legitimate force to maintain security, then a cycle of violence can develop in which violent acts become justified whether as a reaction to the structural violence of deprivation or as self-defence. These acts of violence, lacking legitimate process, can justify further violent reactions. This syllogistic argument justifies the State's monopoly on violence to maintain order and its paternalistic role as guardian of citizens' security. However, and this is particularly relevant in a post-colonial context, the initial legitimacy of the State is here assumed.

The opposing philosophies of power and violence represented by Arendtian and social contract thinking demonstrate the importance of the way violence is analysed to the way that authority, statecraft, and dissent are understood. However, as conceptual theories, their sharp divisions between ideas of power, violence, security, and authority abstract understandings of power away from the messy complex realities in which power and violence co-exist in diverse and fluctuating ways. The ideas of the State formulated in the sixteenth century, or even the mid-twentieth century, may require a radical re-reading (e.g. Fraser, 2004) if they are to be relevant to twenty-first-century political realities in which nation-States are in many cases weaker than multinational corporations and the spaces and means of legitimate political conflict have consequently been reconfigured.

Legitimacy may well be what is at stake in 'fourth generation wars' – the form of warfare first defined in the late 1980s to characterise the development of modern conflicts in which the distinctions between State and non-State actors, and between military and civilian spaces, have

DOI: 10.1057/9781137397362.0006

been blurred (Lind, 2004). Therefore, an assumed distinction between State and non-State in conflict situations may erroneously assume the legitimacy of the former and call into question the legitimacy of the latter (Jones and Rodgers, 2009). In many conflicts, State legitimacy is exactly what is in dispute, and there may be collusion between State and non-State actors, as in cases where paramilitary groups have been shown to be working on behalf of the State.

The State does not immediately have a monopoly on the use of violence – this has to be earned and established – but processes of democratisation have, historically, frequently been extremely violent (Carroll, 2011; Tilly, 2003). The questionable legitimacy of States that have their roots in colonial violence and may represent factional elite rather than public interests (Carroll, 2011) is a source of conflict throughout the world, although these conflicts do not necessarily spill over into violence. The solutions to the crisis of legitimacy implied by social contract theory – to ensure citizens' security, broadly defined, and to have the apparatus in place to have a monopoly on the use of force – can appear simplistic in a globalised world in which nation-States lack the resources to ensure either of these key facets of statehood.

There are political advantages for some to continuing conflicts (Tilly, 2003), and there is also an economic profit for some from continued violence. Understanding the contribution that violence can make to an area's political and economic development is crucial in terms of explaining how long-term epidemic violence perpetuates itself and has a role in the acquisition and maintenance of power (Jones and Rodgers, 2009). This is, for example, true of the arms trade, and in more recent years international funding available to combat violence and 'the war on terror' means that military funding can be seen as being dependent on continued strife (Graham, 2011). If violence has economic beneficiaries, then the resources to keep conflict going will be available – a criticism that has been levied, for example, against the US 'War on Drugs' (Wacquant, 2009).

Political theories of violence have centred on the issues of State and revolutionary violence. Violence in the community, in the family, and on the street is, however, no less political and no less intricately entwined with questions of power. As argued above, violent acts occur when there is a sense that they are justified, and this sense is mediated by discourse, categories, and identities that are culturally situated (Jabri, 1996). Violence comes into play when someone whose structural position gives them power perceives that the use of violence is warranted. Those in

DOI: 10.1057/9781137397362.0006

power can also define what counts as transgression, and when the use of force is warranted, and can also then exercise this force.

Many conflicts are rooted in identity (Sen, 2007). From Northern Ireland to the Middle East, what may have started as conflicts over resources or rights articulate with political tensions that configure along identity lines. It is also the case that conflict forms identity. Those in a hegemonic position shape identity landscapes from their gaze, and the 'others' that are created in the process – indigenous people, blacks, women, religious minorities – are forced to see themselves through the eyes of others, as they are interpellated into the dominant discourse. This power to name and define, which is performed and established as hegemonic groups recreate their identity through everyday cultural practices, is termed 'symbolic violence' (Bourdieu, 1991).

Leadership discourses and who is perceived to be powerful at the State level are themselves culturally situated and recreate and reinforce ideas of power and leadership in community and family spaces (Munck, 2008: 8). As Ehrenreich (cited in Munck, 2008: 8) states, 'it is not only that men make wars, but that wars make men', and 'warrior' tropes of masculinity frame appropriate male behaviour in contexts as distant from direct military action as finance (Maclean, 2015), diplomacy (O'Reilly, 2012), and environmentalism (Connell, 1990). Patriarchal family 'headship' – an idea which justifies patterns of obedience and discipline within households – can underpin intra-familial violence (Chant, 2002). Ideas of 'honour', the transgression of which can justify extreme punishment, frame acts of violence within gangs and within families (Gill et al., 2012). Discussions and analyses of gender-based violence cannot, therefore, be considered in isolation from violence in society more broadly, despite the fact that they are often considered to take place 'in private'. Not only is gender violence framed by discourses of authority, power, transgression, and punishment that are culturally situated, but the home can be a site where such gendered ideologies of power and headship can be recreated and, in turn, frame understandings of war (Cockburn, 2010).

Violence and the city

Violence cannot be understood without understanding power. The power to inflict violence, and the power dynamics implicit in the way that norms, identities, and social relations are defined, frame who can

DOI: 10.1057/9781137397362.0006

be violent and upon whom violence can be inflicted. Struggles for power at the State, non-State, and para-State levels can be seen as conflicts for the right to command obedience and to have a monopoly on the legitimate use of force. Cities are shaped by and shape these power struggles. The urban landscape can be read as a complex multiple over-layering of infrastructures, designs, and architectures from which power struggles and transitions can be inferred (Graham, 2011; Weizman, 2012). The structural violence involved in the deprivation of certain areas, the transport links that prioritise the journeys of the powerful, and the scars of destructive violence perpetrated in the process of establishing power frame urban development. When cities begin a transition to peace, it can be inferred that power dynamics, ideas of behaviour, identity, and leadership have changed, and it might be possible to 'read' this change in the cityscape.

Studies of peacetime violence, both individual and collective, have tended to focus on cities, where the rapid, and accelerating, urbanisation of the twentieth century has engendered spaces of high crime, gang-related violence, and terrorist assaults. Each of the cities that have been the subject of these investigations is, of course, unique, and offers its own individual case, but there are some consistencies in the features of cities that have tended to host high levels of violence. Inequality and exclusion are common themes across these studies (Winton, 2004), but the ghettoised violence associated with North American cities and the related cycles of exclusion, surveillance, and incarceration (Wacquant, 2009) are fundamentally different from the violence associated with post-Apartheid South Africa or the narco-related violence of Mexico. As Robinson (2006) advises, urbanists would do well to analyse differences, as much as similarities, and to resist the dominance of a Northern model in urban theorising.

Most analyses of urban violence and the corresponding remedies are framed by social contract theories, as outlined above. Particularly in a transition context, it can appear that violence has emerged out of a power vacuum and the inability of a State to secure its monopoly on the use of force. However, critics of this approach indicate the importance of taking historical trajectory into account, and of considering violence as a continuation of pre-existing power structures that may be rendered invisible if the focus is on the absence of a Weberian State. Looking for correlations between factors that define the urban – population density, extent and patterns of (un)employment, consumption, and production – can begin to illustrate why so much peacetime violence occurs in cities. The technical solutions that have been suggested as a result generally resonate with market-led modernisation projects, and, although arguably more progressive than militarisation, may reaffirm as well as challenge the powers behind urban structural violence. However, this approach risks erasing the historical, social, and economic context unique to each city, and so misconstruing the political processes that continue to cause inequality, marginalisation, and violence.

Explorations of urban violence in the context of the transition to democracy have studied the various violent actors that gain power in the 'absence' (in the conception of social contract theory) of a legitimate, extended, and capable State, and how these political dynamics engage with the structural violence present in highly unequal cities. The characteristics of political transformation – the presence of para-State and paramilitary actors and a high number of arms – do not disappear once a transition to democracy has been agreed upon. The fear and distrust created by a repressive State, and the collusion between violent groups, render State legitimacy inherently questionable and difficult to achieve (Winton, 2004). The reform of the police, the demobilisation of armed actors, and the processes to recognise historical, political, and economic grievances that are necessary in transition contexts can themselves catalyse violence.

Transition situations can create a climate of insecurity and fear that spills beyond political conflicts per se to a context in which violence is justified in terms of defence and survival. Armed groups, despite demobilising, have been found to regroup in criminal organisations (Winton, 2004), and the availability of arms, despite various amnesties, may not diminish. The relationship between local armed actors – including paramilitary and para-State organisations with political justifications for their actions, as well as organised crime and gangs – and legitimate forces is also a factor in the development of urban violence. Although the police are primarily conceived of as the executive arm of the State's monopoly on the use of legitimate force, they are often seen to be the main perpetrators of illegitimate violence (Winton, 2004). Their collusion with armed groups ranges from practical recognition of the power that armed actors have and the need to link up with them to be effective, to outright corruption. Similarly, the justice system is crucial in distinguishing legitimate use of force from illegitimate power struggles or extra-judicial killings, but may, for reasons of corruption or lack of power, be unable to

DOI: 10.1057/9781137397362.0006

fulfil that role systematically and effectively. However, a complete disassociation between local armed actors and the State has also been seen to increase armed actors' power and therefore the potential for violence (Moncada, 2013).

Youth gangs have been argued to take on State or community functions in contexts where State authority is 'fragile', and there is a strong correlation between 'violence-affected urban spaces and gang consolidation, size and distribution' (Rodgers and Muggah, 2009: 304). Gangs have hierarchical structures, rituals, and norms that distinguish them from simple agglomerations of isolated youths and can have social and political aims. Gangs are often defined territorially and have an 'institutional continuity that is independent of their membership' (Rodgers and Muggah, 2009: 302). The formation of gangs is associated with disenfranchised and excluded young men who can find there the identity, affirmation, and employment which is denied to them in mainstream society. The vast majority of gang members are young men between the ages of 18 and 34, and members of this demographic are also most likely to be victims of homicide. Women are also involved, but gang symbolism recreates hyper-masculine ideals, which go on to be glorified in pop culture around the world, from gangster rap to the infamous Mexican *narco-corridos*, which glorify the heinous, and frequently misogynist, violence associated with the drugs trade.

One of the variables most strongly statistically correlated with violence is the size and speed of growth of a city. Larger cities tend to be more violent than smaller ones. This is not due to size per se, but rather related to the greater concentrations of wealth and levels of exclusion to be found in large cities, and, crucially, the speed of growth, which has consistently been found to be a strong predictor of violence in cities (Muggah and Savage, 2012). The causal mechanism behind this correlation is debatable and depends on the specific local historical, political, and economic context. Rapid growth could be the result of economic migration – rural–urban, regional, or international migration. If a city has grown quickly, then one would expect the structural violence of poverty, exclusion, and inequality to increase as well. The kinship-based traditional authority, surveillance, and control that have kept order in rural communities may not pertain in the city. The breakdown of 'peer surveillance' in this way speaks to the connection between high levels of 'social capital' – basically trust networks and connections – and low levels of violence. However, anthropological work that shows how such

DOI: 10.1057/9781137397362.0006

familial and community controls are maintained after migration could challenge or at least nuance this conclusion (e.g. Koch, 2006).

Inequality related to rapid city growth tends to be associated with areas of high urban density, high levels of deprivation, and poor levels of infrastructural connectivity. These areas are variously, and controversially, called 'informal settlements', 'slums', or '*favelas*', and levels of urban violence are in some cases exponentially higher in these areas. If urban poverty is seen to be related to urban violence, richer neighbourhoods opt to securitise, and an equivalent 'ghettoisation' of the rich occurs (Atkinson, 2006), as the influence of elite priorities on planning and the availability of private security and 'gated communities' allow those with means to segregate themselves away from the problems of urban violence, hence compounding the inequality and exclusion which may well underpin them.

Given its associations with inequality and deprivation, violence is considered a development issue (Moser and McIlwaine, 2006). However, the assumption that modernisation and economic development will ameliorate violence is difficult to maintain. Market-led development, whilst being effective at controlling inflation and generating growth, has been shown to be limited in its ability to address inequality and exclusion, and has in many places vastly exacerbated these problems. The specific ways in which the city is inserted into the global economy will, however, mediate these effects (Moncada, 2013). Whilst it has been claimed that the employment generated by market-led growth can address the causes of violence (World Bank, 2010), certain areas of high violence have been directly associated with processes of globalisation, for example the victims of femicide in Ciudad Juárez have tended to work in the assembly-line plants along the border (Wright, 2004). This creates a contradiction, noted by Winton (2004: 179), that 'while violence is a considerable barrier to development, the development process itself has been instrumental in both producing and shaping new forms of urban violence in the South'.

The illicit drugs economy has been closely associated with violence around the globe, but particularly in Latin America and the Caribbean (Winton, 2004). Narco-traffic provides the profit motives and, crucially, the resources for violence to continue, and conflict between rival cartels, associated gang violence, and disputes over routes have resulted in spectacular violence that has in some areas become endemic. The vast wealth associated with narco-trafficking has led to cartels being able to compete

DOI: 10.1057/9781137397362.0006

on a level with the State in terms of military force, and stepping into the State's role of security enforcer (Ceballos Melguizo and Cronshaw, 2001). Whilst the human and social costs of narco-related violence are indisputable, it is difficult not to accept the role that drugs have had in economic development. Money laundering has resulted in architectural, institutional, and infrastructural developments that have shaped city and national economies, although clearly on extremely problematic grounds (Jones and Rodgers, 2011). The very 'success' of narco-violence has ensured its continuance in the political fabric of countries unfortunate enough to be on drugs trail from producer countries to market – predominantly North America and Western Europe.

Policies to deal with urban violence

Since the turn of the century, security analysts have gone further than the accepted assertion that most peacetime violence occurs in cities, to claim that urban violence outweighs that found in war and that security and counter-insurgency agencies need to re-focus their objectives on urban violence (Muggah, 2013). The problem of violence in cities has also been cast as a problem for development (Moser and McIlwaine, 2006), given the costs to health care systems and the drain on production. Policies to reduce urban violence have ranged from securitisation to job creation and have involved an array of national and international agencies. Violence has also become an issue for urban planning. Not only does the urban landscape show the scars of urban violence, but urban infrastructure, design, and architecture have been used as tools in addressing the causes, as well as mitigating the effects, of urban violence.

Cities have become the sites of military security interventions. This reflects the development of fourth generation warfare, in which bellicose geopolitics is played out in 'low-intensity conflicts' in civilian areas, rather than on the battleground (Graham, 2011). Terrorist attacks on 'global cities' are used most often to justify a militarised response, but military approaches, personnel, and, most importantly, budgets have been used in cities around the world to fight various 'wars' on terrorism, drugs, and poverty. Cities such as Ciudad Juárez, Rio de Janeiro, Cape Town, and London have all seen military action on civilian populations that have been known variously as 'pacification', 'stabilisation', or 'consolidation' (Muggah, 2013).

DOI: 10.1057/9781137397362.0006

Military interventions in urban violence correspond with an association of violence with security. Shoring up the State's monopoly on violence is seen to be a rational step in the context of a 'failed State' which is not able to provide or secure security. This metaphor has been extended to the urban scale, with a discourse of 'fragile cities' framing security and development interventions. Military interventions on these grounds have been paralleled by changes in the way that humanitarian assistance is provided; for example, the Red Cross has extended its wartime operations to cities in countries that are not 'at war' but have high rates of urban violence (Bernal-Franco and Navas-Caputo, 2013; Muggah and Savage, 2012). These military interventions may involve institutional strengthening and to some extent may address the social exclusions underpinning violence, as well as quelling it. However, politically, such interventions may shore up elite power, repress legitimate resistance, and further confuse the question of which actors have the right to use force. Moreover, it has been argued that militarisation is taking place in a global political-economic context in which the ever-expanding security–industrial nexus is itself dependent on ongoing conflict situations (Graham, 2011).

The built environment and violence are related in terms of how violence has changed the city, and also how the structures of the city have affected violence. Some studies have suggested, for instance, that broken windows and dilapidated buildings are not only the consequence of violence but perhaps a cause (Newman, 1973). Equally, the structural violence of exclusion and inequality can have its roots in a city's geography and infrastructure. Violence also shapes cities in terms of the surveillance and security measures that may be taken to deal with it from the point of view of those in power. Whilst poorer neighbourhoods may become peppered with CCTV cameras and other mechanisms of surveillance, richer areas are increasingly secluding themselves from any notion of the 'public' (Atkinson, 2006). In the name of security, the spaces of those in power are becoming more isolated and protected, whilst poorer people are under more scrutiny. Although this might protect certain people from violence, it increases the structural conditions that may have caused it in the first place.

Job creation and market-led development are also being cast as players in the fight against urban violence. This approach has been adopted prominently by the World Bank, which, on the basis of interviews with people in violent communities, identifies unemployment as being

DOI: 10.1057/9781137397362.0006

perceived as the strongest cause of violence. The most recommended policy intervention is market-led growth, which also involves infrastructural investment to allow the market to extend to poorer areas of the city and investment to build up the connections between producers, retailers, and consumers (World Bank, 2010).

Community-based preventive interventions also focus on job creation, and often involve education and training for jobs and interventions designed to foster an entrepreneurial spirit. These interventions are primarily targeted at youths in violent communities, who are perceived as being most at risk from violence and most likely to be caught up in the institutions presumed to perpetuate it – namely, gangs. Community interventions also focus on building trust and social capital. Strategies to achieve this have included, the use of participatory budgets to make the community responsible for the public investments and works carried out there, community art exhibitions, and collective memory exercises (Moser and McIlwaine, 2004).

At each level, from global security to community work, the urban landscape is an inherent part of attempts to address urban violence. UN Habitat has emphasised the connections between urban planning, crime, and violence, pointing out that 'poor urban planning, design and management have increasingly been cited as playing a role in the shaping of urban environments that put citizens and property at risk', and it cites research showing that 'physical design and management of the built environment play a role ... in diminishing opportunities for crime and violence' (UN Human Settlements Programme, 2007). However, with the exception of certain projects involving participation at the community level, the recommendations regarding the built environment tend to be based on statistical analyses of the causes of violence, and the conclusions tend to recommend the infrastructure and modernisation projects associated with market-led development. Assessments focus on the outputs and impact of infrastructural projects, and hence measures for dealing with urban violence are presented as a technical fix that can be taken up in countries with similar issues, regardless of historical background or political context.

Urban architecture is also a method of control. From theorisations of panopticism to the design of park benches, urban design has played a central role in how populations are governed (Stienen, 2009). Examples of urban design motivated by the need to control citizen by segregation and surveillance abound. Haussman's boulevards in Paris were aimed at

DOI: 10.1057/9781137397362.0006

minimising the potential for disruptive protests (Douglas, 2008), and in Cardiff pink lighting has been used to discourage 'unruly' teenagers (BBC, 2012). Architecture is a 'technology of power', and although the extension of infrastructure to excluded populations can address barriers to participation and unequal access to resources, it can also be seen as an extension of the power of elites and the State.

Cities are shaped by capital and elites – whether in how castles have been fortified, how social housing has been built to support a workforce, or how gated communities have been created to ensure the security of those with means. The dynamics behind these landscapes include public policy as well as private interests and proclivities, as the aesthetics of city development are also guided by elite tastes. However, cities are also shaped by resistance to these dynamics (Stienen, 2009). Understanding the spaces of the city in terms of how they reflect and create power would, with reference to analyses of the relationship between urban planning and violence, shift the focus from the outputs and impacts to the political processes behind how the city is being designed (McCann, 2002) and to who has the 'right to the city' (Purcell, 2002; McCann, 2002).

One way to address this is to promote community participation in urban planning. However, given the dominance of policies associated with modernisation and the view that urban planning is a technical fix, it may be difficult for the voices of community members to have a meaningful influence on these processes. Whilst community participation can improve the appropriateness of the intervention to the local area, it has been argued that there is a 'post-political' consensus in urban planning that allows a conflict-free, technical consensus to emerge despite the importance of participation and partnership being highlighted as part of this very consensus (Raco, 2013). As Lefebvre claims, 'the ideology of participation enables us to have the acquiescence of interested and concerned people at a small price. After a more or less elaborate pretence at information and social activity, they return to their tranquillity and retirement' (cited in McCann, 2002: 78).

Conclusion

Approaches to the analysis of violence range in scale from the individual psychology of the perpetrator to the structural factors that correlate with violence at the city and national levels. The contention of this chapter is

DOI: 10.1057/9781137397362.0006

that violence needs to be understood in terms of processes of acquiring and retaining power, and that psychological and structural approaches – prominent in policy documents and popular debate on the subject – are insufficient as they ignore social, economic, and political context. Whilst the establishment of correlations of violence with inequality and exclusion foregrounds the importance of socioeconomic structures, it can oversimplify the causal relationship involved (often adopting the terms of the social contract) and does not sufficiently take into account the historical, political, and discursive processes behind high levels of inequality. Although these correlations permit a recognition of structural violence and the idea that inequality or exclusion is a violence in itself, they can also support the further stigmatisation of marginalised areas and so increase the segregation which is associated with urban violence. Understanding urban violence requires an analysis that can situate the phenomenon in its material, historical, and discursive context, and examine the role that violence has in the power struggles and political processes that have shaped the city. Local discourses of identity and culturally constructed ideas of power and leadership are as important to explaining how violence has entered into the 'common sense' of how to achieve political aims as the historical and economic context underpinning the marginalisation, inequality, and rapid growth that have been correlated with urban violence, but do not determine its presence.

In the context of transition to democracy, which is also associated with urban violence, the assumption of a legitimate State, and the equally often assumed neat division between formal and informal powers, need to be challenged. Examining the role that violence has had in establishing competing powers, and the interests that its continuance serves, is important to understanding the possibilities of establishing a State monopoly on the use of force and whether reinforcing formal State powers will serve to perpetuate the exclusions underpinning long-term endemic violence. A framework that recognises violence as the perpetuation of certain social and political norms, rather than as a 'breakdown' in the social fabric or a 'power vacuum', renders these dynamics visible. In the context of urban violence, this means looking at how violent actors have gained power, how violence has entered into the norms of everyday life, and normative ideas of how political leadership is performed. Inequality and exclusion do not necessarily lead to violence, but in certain contexts they may facilitate the rise to power of armed groups

DOI: 10.1057/9781137397362.0006

who are able to provide protection and security in areas where formal powers represent factional elites rather than the public interest.

A contextualised, place-specific approach shifts the focus of policies designed to address urban violence from technical interventions, typically infrastructure projects, to the political processes behind how these policies are developed and the effects that they have on the political fabric of the city. Inequality and exclusion are not sufficient conditions for urban violence, although they are important factors in its development. Urban violence results from the political processes that have created these exclusions, and in turn from the way that inequality and exclusion maintain violence as part of political process.

The next chapter explores the historical and political process behind the long-term endemic violence in Medellín. Medellín exhibits all the factors correlated with urban violence – high levels of inequality and exclusion, rapid city growth, and being in the midst of political transition to democracy. However, the political spaces and processes that developed are the result of long-term historical conflicts and tensions that have led to violence being part of the 'common sense' of politics and everyday life in the city. Economic hardship, exclusion, and exclusive elites have created a political landscape that constitutes structural violence, that has legitimated violence from a variety of political perspectives, and that has underpinned collusion between supposedly formal State forces and other armed actors. The processes and policies of social urbanism need to be seen in this context.

DOI: 10.1057/9781137397362.0006

2
Medellín: The Most Violent City in the World

Abstract: *Throughout the twentieth century, Colombia was plagued by violence, as a bitter civil war was fought between the Liberal and Conservative parties, over a period which also saw the formation of Marxist guerrilla groups and paramilitary groups. However, violence in Medellín in the 1980s greatly exceeded levels of violence in the rest of the country and is particularly associated with the rise to power of Pablo Escobar and his Medellín Cartel. This chapter analyses the factors involved in Medellín's violence in terms of how violence became part of the processes via which power and authority were gained in the city. High levels of inequality, insecurity, and exclusion contributed to a context in which the cartel, urban militia, and paramilitary groups were able to gain power by promising work, upward mobility, and security. However, the role of the State in direct military action in certain civilian areas, political populism, and a blurring of formal and informal politics, as well as legitimate and illegitimate authority, are crucial and often overlooked factors in understanding Medellín's violence.*

Keywords: Colombian history; guerrilla groups; La Violencia; narco-traffic; paramilitaries; urban violence

Maclean, Kate. *Social Urbanism and the Politics of Violence: The Medellín Miracle.* Basingstoke: Palgrave Macmillan, 2015. DOI: 10.1057/9781137397362.0007.

...ultidimensional violence encompasses Colombia's long-
...l conflict, Marxist guerrilla movements in rural areas, Marxist
...rban areas, paramilitary forces, and the State, as well as, of
...co-related violence and the actions of the notorious Medellín
Cartel. Medellín, as has been found with other violent cities, has high levels
of inequality and exclusion, and the city grew rapidly over the latter half of
the twentieth century. The predominant narrative is that these structural
issues have left spaces where the need to provide security, in terms of
protection from violence and assurance of broader social rights, has fallen
to non-State armed actors, who have used the unwillingness and inability
of formal political powers to fulfil this need to gain power. This discourse
has been used by leftist militia, paramilitary groups, and the cartel, all of
whom have been able to gain support among people in the excluded *comunas* (similar to city boroughs or districts) of Medellín by stepping into the
apparent breach left by the State. However, it would be erroneous to think
in terms of a power vacuum here. As discussed in the previous chapter,
formal political power is often present in numerous and troubling ways
in such areas, and in particular the vertical style of political power and the
proximity of formal and informal armed actors has meant that the actions
of political leaders have enabled the prominence of violence in the political
process, rather than this happening in the State's 'absence'.

The emergence of violence as an endemic characteristic of the
way that power is attained, maintained, and reproduced cannot be
understood without putting inequality and exclusion in the city into
historical, social, and political perspective. Vulnerability to violence is
highly spatially segregated in Medellín. The hillsides of the city to the
northeast and northwest, which developed over the latter half of the
twentieth century to house migrants fleeing the violence of Colombia's
civil conflict or seeking a better living in what is referred to locally as
the 'the economic magnet' that is Medellín, are the locus of much of
the violence, whilst richer areas to the south have been able to secure
themselves. Understanding violence in this city involves understanding
its geography and the political spaces that formed Medellín's 'multiple
theatres of violence' (Pécaut, 1999).

This chapter explores the reasons behind the rapid growth and high
rates of inequality in Medellín, in order to paint a fuller picture of the
political spaces that opened up to allow extremely violent actors to gain
power. The reasons for migration to the city and the historical background to protectionist elite attitudes allow a fuller picture to emerge of

DOI: 10.1057/9781137397362.0007

how armed groups encompassing the drugs cartels, urban militia, paramilitaries, and criminal gangs, as well as the State, gained and maintained power through violence, to the point that it became 'banal'. The political violence of the civil conflict, the structural violence of inequality, and the social, everyday violence, framed by interpretations of what it means to be powerful, to be a leader, or to have authority, interact to form spaces in which violence is recreated as a way to attain and maintain power. From the housing developments provided by Pablo Escobar in the poorest areas of the city to the bullet holes from the strafing of the Colombian military's attack on militia strongholds on the hillsides, Medellín's urban landscape bears the scars not only of the violence but also of the political struggles and processes that perpetuated it.

Rapid growth, inequality, gangs, and narco-traffic

Medellín's population increased exponentially after the 1950s, from 275,000 in 1952 to 1.3 million by the late 1970s (Lowenthal and Rojas Mejía, 2010). It is a highly unequal city, standing out even among other Colombian cities as having the highest Gini coefficient (El Espectador, 2013). In 1991, at the peak of the violence, Medellín's Gini coefficient was 0.51, whilst the average for other leading cities was 0.47 (Roldán, 1999). Much of the inequality is related not only to the city's rapid growth but also to the reaction, over decades, of the city's leaders to the influx of people, many of whom were fleeing violence in rural areas. Medellín's development over the second half of the twentieth century aimed to protect the existing residents, a strategy that was stewarded by the city's 'oligarchic' elites (Browitt, 2001). The result is a highly unequal landscape that underpins the violence for which Medellín is known.

Two main factors have spurred migration to Medellín: the political violence that plagued Colombia throughout the late twentieth century and economic migration in search of work in Medellín's industries. In addition to this regional migration, the majority of intra-urban displacement in Colombia takes place in Medellín (Carrillo, 2009). Since the 1980s and 1990s, when the allegiances and politics most associated with Colombia's rural violence began to be recreated in the city, intra-urban displacement has grown. Affiliation to certain political groups in certain areas – for example, guerrilla, criminal, or paramilitary groups – can lead to violent threats that necessitate a move to a different part of the city.

DOI: 10.1057/9781137397362.0007

Although the distances involved are short, the material and emotional loss is not diminished, and this phenomenon exacerbates inequality as well as breaking down communities and possibilities for cooperation.

Medellín is characterised by the way inequality and poverty are distributed spatially in the city. It is divided into 16 *comunas* that are known by their number as well as their name (Figure 2). The wealthiest area, El Poblado, boasts enormous, hyper-modern shopping malls and exclusive boutiques and restaurants, as well as the city's private university, EAFIT. Although officially El Poblado is the 14th *comuna* of Medellín, it is rarely described as such, as the word *comuna* tends to be associated with the poorer areas of the city. The other *comunas* are referred to as being either in the northeast or northwest, the former being associated more with rural immigration and the latter with economic migration to the city. The two most notorious neighbourhoods are Comuna 13, also known as San Javier, and Comuna 1, in which is found the neighbourhood – *barrio* – of Santo Domingo. These areas were, and in many ways continue to be, particularly beset by the narco-, paramilitary, and urban militia violence in the city.

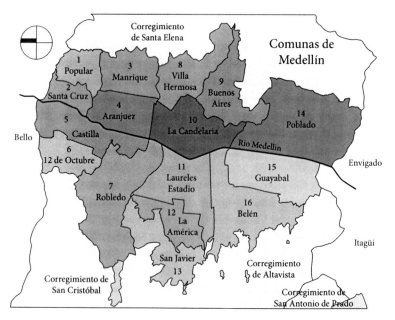

FIGURE 2 *Map of the* comunas *of Medellín*

Source: By SajoR (own work) [public domain], via Wikimedia Commons, http://commons. wikimedia.org/wiki/File%3AComunas_de_Medellín.png.

Not shown in Figure 2 are the 'invisible borders' marking out the territories of the different factions that control security, moral order, and narco-traffic in these areas: the urban militia, paramilitary groups, criminal gangs, and drug cartels – or, according to some living in the *comunas*, 'kids with guns'. It is extraordinarily difficult to live in these areas without being in some sense aligned with one of these groups, who effectively run the community. Those suspected of disloyalty, which could include everyday activities such as being on the wrong side of these invisible lines or being part of an NGO project, will be threatened with violence if they do not leave the area within a specified time – often 24 hours.

Although Medellín is in many senses a 'textbook' violent city, because of its rapid growth and inequality, and also high levels of gang membership, it is clear that without an understanding of the processes via which these phenomena have occurred, their relationship with widespread violence cannot be understood. The role of Colombia's long-running civil conflicts, the formation of its elites, and broader economic factors also come into play in terms not only of understanding why the city has developed as it has, but also of linking these factors to the question of how violence became endemic in Medellín's political processes. This is not because of the 'absence' of a State, which has a problematic presence in violent areas (Gutiérrez and Jaramillo, 2004), or a 'breakdown' in social order, but rather because of the way political and discursive justifications for violence are recreated.

Elites

The twentieth century in Colombia was dominated by conflict between elite groups who, although bitter and violent rivals, have been notably effective, particularly in comparison with other Latin American countries, at retaining their collective hold on formal power. The Liberal and Conservative political parties in Colombia were, until 2003, a duopoly who represented exclusive, colonial elites. These two parties have been fierce and violent rivals, plunging the country into two civil wars since the late nineteenth century, the Thousand Days War (1899–1903) and the undeclared civil war La Violencia (1948–1953) (Roldán, 1997). The latter of these conflicts continues to mark the Colombian political landscape. Triggered by the assassination of Liberal presidential candidate Jorge

DOI: 10.1057/9781137397362.0007

Eliecer Gaitan in 1948, La Violencia spread from Bogotá to become a five-year conflict between Conservative and Liberal factions that was played out largely in rural areas of Colombia, during which people were killed because of their party allegiances (Carroll, 2011; LaRosa and Mejía, 2012).

It is a characteristic of feuds between elite groups in Colombia that they are brought together in the face of external threats, and the pacts developed in the face of such threats have been key to elites' retention of power. In 1953, Colombia's first military coup of the twentieth century occurred, lead by General Gustavo Rojas Pinilla. The rise of the military spurred the Liberals and Conservatives into agreeing a resolution to La Violencia (Roldán, 2002). The resolution was a pact between the two political parties that they would alternate in political office, an agreement known as the Frente Nacional [the National Front]. The National Front lasted from 1958 to 1974 and effectively locked out any potential representation from other political affiliations or persuasions. The years following the signing of this pact saw the birth of various Marxist guerrilla groups, best known among which are the Fuerzas Armadas Revolucionarias de Colombia [Revolutionary Armed Forces of Colombia – FARC], Ejército de Liberación Nacional [National Liberation Army – ELN], and the Movimiento 19 de Abril [Movement of the 19th of April – M19]. The same period witnessed the rise of paramilitary forces, which the government of the time encouraged, allegedly on advice from the United States, in order to quell the rise of communist groups in rural areas (Bejarano and Leongómez, 2002). In 1962, Plan Lazo, a State counter-insurgency programme that facilitated the provision of armaments to paramilitary 'civilian defence' groups, was put into action, laying the foundations for the paramilitarism of the 1990s (NACLA, 2009).

Although it has been argued that Medellín was less affected by La Violencia than other cities (Roldán, 2002), the legacy of this vicious political conflict in terms of the ongoing conflict between State, paramilitary, and guerrilla forces, exclusivity of political elites, and lack of distinction between legitimate and illegitimate violence has had a strong impact on the propensity for violence in Medellín. The social and economic exclusion of the *comunas* has been compounded by a political system that does not incentivise representation. As such, these areas have been ripe for exploitation by powerful leaders from cartels, militia, and paramilitary factions, who have been able to provide 'security' in a manner indistinguishable from that of formal political powers (Gutiérrez and Jaramillo,

DOI: 10.1057/9781137397362.0007

2004). Moreover, this is recreated in ideas of power and leadership that can be seen not only in the aggression of leaders but also in the culture of what it means to be respected in the community and at home.

The stability and exclusivity of elite political leaders in Medellín, reinforced by the national-level duopoly of the Liberal and Conservative parties, led to the underdevelopment of structures that would encourage political participation and deepen democracy. Vertical relationships of patronage shape political representation in the city. Politicians have historically been seen as bestowers of rights rather than representatives or leaders who support civic and political rights to critical participation. For example, politicians who held rallies in the city would use their power to give gifts to the community or respond to individual demands, in a style of representation that mirrors the vertical relationships of patronage and clientelism that are familiar aspects of the Latin American political landscape (Auyero, 2000). Such paternalist methods are argued to undermine democracy and encourage a style of personal leadership known as 'caudillo' (De la Torre, 2010), in which authority is kept with one, often militaristic, leader. As a consequence, the development of democratic checks and balances and associated institutions is attenuated. This political culture fails to distinguish legitimate power, and informal political actors were able to exploit the poverty and exclusion of the comunas in the same way as formal political actors because of the lack of institutional structure to underpin legitimate political forces.

The power-brokers in Medellín have traditionally been an economic bourgeoisie who have managed to keep wealth in their families for generations, and certain surnames recur throughout the region's political and economic history (Hylton, 2007; Restrepo Santamaria, 2011). Medellín's position as the centre of Colombia's industrialisation, particularly in textiles, was built upon the success of these entrepreneurial elite families in the mining and coffee booms. The development of factories did bring employment and a higher standard of living to many, and a value of which Antioquian elites are particularly proud is the importance of investing in one's people. It is argued that commitment from elites and the tradition of patronage encouraged by their strict Catholicism allowed Antioquia to become one of the most inventive and economically effective areas of South America (Restrepo Santamaria, 2011).

However, political opinion over the role of elites in establishing the preconditions for the violence in Medellín is divided. Whilst some consider that the exclusivity of the region's economic elites in effect

DOI: 10.1057/9781137397362.0007

protected economic leaders from infiltration by criminal or illegitimate elements, others judge that the mechanisms for maintaining this exclusivity compounded the exclusion which underpins the emergence of violence and criminality (Roldán, 1997). As well as the inequality and exclusion which this perpetuates, the patronage for which the region is famed affirms vertical power relations, as is illustrated by the oft-quoted phrase '*La caridad consuela, pero no cuestiona*' ['Charity comforts, but does not challenge'].

Particularly characteristic of Medellín's elites is their fear of takeover by competitors in Bogotá. Coupled with a strong sense of regional identity and pride, this fear led to the development of several corporations designed explicitly to ward off the threat of takeover by outsiders. These groups include the powerful Grupo Empresarial Antioqueño [Antioquian Business Group – GEA], also known as the Sindicato Antioqueño. The GEA was formed in the 1970s when it was perceived that businesses from Bogotá were taking over Antioquian companies by buying up a majority of the shares (*El Colombiano*, 2011). When certain iconic Antioquian companies were bought up in this way – including the Medellín-based textiles company Coltejer and the National Chocolate Company, *Nacional de Chocolates* – business leaders decided to form conglomerates to protect 'regional' businesses. This was achieved by key business leaders from Antioquian companies exchanging shares in order to keep out 'foreign' interests – a defensive business manoeuvre that became known as the '*enroque paisa*'.[1]

Unlike in other Colombian cities that were affected by narco-traffic, in Medellín the claim is that traditional businesses were not permeated by the cartel. The exclusionary social networks, known as '*roscas*', the protectionist business manoeuvres to keep out competition from Bogotá, and the social exclusivity of elites all ensured that the cartel was kept at bay. A story that has entered into the folklore of Medellín is that at the height of his wealth – and in the 1980s he was worth more than US$2 billion (Forbes, 2012) – Pablo Escobar was turned away from the country club in the elite neighbourhood of El Poblado because he 'wasn't the right sort'. His gauche manners and dress betrayed his lower-class background, and although he was involved politically and economically with the city's power-brokers at that time, he was not allowed to enter their cultural spaces. Cultural dynamics did indeed divide the Medellín Cartel from the circles of Medellín business, unlike in Cali, for example, where the cartel was known as 'The Cali Gentlemen' and allegedly had a far closer

DOI: 10.1057/9781137397362.0007

relationship with formal businesses. As one of the leaders of Medellín's cultural industries affirmed, 'At the time they [business elites] were desperate to get in with the mafia – they were the ones with the money! If you had your house for sale, the ideal was if someone came to look at it from the cartel – they'd offer you triple the asking price on the spot! I tell you the only reason that lot were excluded was their bad taste.'[2]

Many hold that, given the vast wealth of Escobar's cartel, Medellín's economy was *necessarily* affected. This position is, however, controversial, and it has been argued that narco-traffic accounts for a minute percentage of Colombian GDP. Nevertheless, Pablo Escobar's wealth had a particular impact on the economy of Medellín. Whilst the region's traditional businesses, owned by prominent Antioquian families, were not affected, other businesses, notably in the construction industry and commerce, were. It is also alleged that these industries were complicit in money laundering for the cartel (Carroll, 2011). There are areas of Medellín – from the Barrio Pablo Escobar, a neighbourhood of houses that Escobar built in Comuna 9 that remains to this day, to downtown shopping malls – that are rumoured to have been developed using capital that came from narco-traffic.

Although economically powerful families in Antioquia are also characterised by a commitment to investing in their workers, this paternalist approach can be argued to exacerbate exclusion (Hylton, 2007). Patronage instigated a vertical method of social control, which broke down when the city's industries were badly affected by recession (Ceballos Melguizo and Cronshaw, 2001). As social rights such as housing and education were also dependent on employment, the effects of recession and de-industrialisation associated with the economic crisis of the 1980s, and felt particularly harshly in industrial Medellín, were in some cases catastrophic. The unemployment rate in Medellín varied from 14 to 17 per cent between 1982 and 1988, but much more significant was the size of the informal economy, which is estimated to have provided more than 50 per cent of employment throughout the 1980s (Betancur, 2007). Migration from rural areas continued apace during the 1980s and 1990s, despite the growing rates of poverty and violence, and the poorer areas to the north and northeast of the city were dominated by informal livelihoods – from petty commerce to sex work and involvement in criminal gangs and cartels.

Formal politics in Medellín stands out in the main for the pragmatism of its formal political leaders in terms of forming strategic alliances, and

DOI: 10.1057/9781137397362.0007

high levels of corruption (Carroll, 2011; Gutiérrez and Jaramillo, 2004). The pragmatism has perhaps shielded Medellín from certain kinds of political violence, but at the same time arguably contributed to exclusion. Corruption can be usefully categorised into two forms: the nepotism and patronage that ensured the continuity of patrimonial elites in power, and bribery, corruption, and influence from illegitimate political actors. There was no shortage of bribery and corruption in Medellín politics during the 1980s, due not least to the presence of 'narco-politics' and collusion with the Medellín Cartel (Filippone, 1994). This was a clear source of power for informal political actors that further eroded the distinction between legitimate and illegitimate politics. Nevertheless, the nepotism and pragmatism characteristic of formal political practice in the city also engendered power structures that were ripe for abuse.

State, militia, paramilitaries, cartels, and criminal gangs

The armed groups involved in Medellín's violence, who were able to gain power in the city and not only perpetrate violence but also make it an inherent part of the city's politics, came from opposed political angles. What they had in common, however, was the ability to exploit the poverty and exclusion of the *comunas* by offering hopes for social mobility and being able to provide security in areas which formal political actors had neglected. The ways, means, and aims were distinct, but the power bases that all were able to establish depended on the structural exclusion of the *comunas*, the impermeability of elite positions, and the insecurity that led to a situation in which violence was deemed to necessitate violence, in a context where the boundaries of 'legitimate' force were unclear.

Cocaine, the cartels, and 'narco-terrorism'

The violence in Medellín specifically is most closely associated with the Medellín Cartel, and its leader Pablo Escobar. Escobar's ferocious violence was one element of the way in which the cartel gained and maintained power, but its bases were much broader than that. Escobar had support in certain *comunas* as a leader who understood the plight of poor people and who also was in a position to provide housing and security. His vast wealth made him at one point the seventh richest man on Earth (Forbes, 2012) and allowed him to compete, in terms of the weaponry and

DOI: 10.1057/9781137397362.0007

influence that money can buy, on a level with the Colombian State. It is worth remembering that despite his huge personal influence, Medellín's violence increased after Escobar's death; more pertinent than the association of the problem entirely with one individual is the process by which one man could have accumulated that much power to abuse.

The Colombian drug cartels gained power in the late 1970s and early 1980s. Various cartels were formed at this time, and the main rival to the Medellín Cartel was the Cali Cartel, based in the city of the same name. The Medellín Cartel was by far the most profitable and the most violent, and at its height controlled 60 per cent of the world's cocaine (Filippone, 1994). There are several reasons Medellín became the location of the world's largest and most violent drug cartel. First, Medellín's geographical position was perfect in terms of smuggling routes into the United States. Medellín was well positioned for access to routes across the Caribbean and overland via Mexico. Second, there was a history of smuggling in Medellín. In the 1960s, the centres of drug smuggling were Cuba for cocaine and Mexico for marijuana. As these operations diminished, owing to various political factors, including successful operations by the United States, both trades moved towards Colombia. Finally, it is alleged that alliances that the cartel was able to build with paramilitary and formal powers, crucially to protect and enable the routes used for transport, allowed the trade to flourish in Medellín (Hylton, 2006, 2007; Tubb, 2013).

The main leaders of the Medellín Cartel were Pablo Escobar, Carlos Lehder, and the Ochoa brothers. Escobar was from a humble background and was a small-time crook, stealing and re-selling gravestones, until he discovered the possibilities in smuggling cocaine. He joined forces with the three Ochoa brothers, sons of an affluent cattle-ranching family, and the smuggler Carlos Lehder. When Lehder met the smuggler George Jung (aka 'Boston George'') in jail, they hatched a plan to bring cocaine over in planeloads rather than having 'mules' bring small amounts across the border. According to US Attorney Robert Merckle, 'Lehder was to cocaine trafficking what Henry Ford was to automobiles' (Filippone, 1994: 325). This change in strategy revolutionised the cocaine industry and brought the people who controlled it unimaginable profits.

The cartel was willing and able to spend its wealth on the excluded in ways that the elites of the city were not. They built housing, invested in popular attractions such as football pitches, and sponsored one of Medellín's main football teams (Gugliotta and Leen, 2011; Skaperdas,

2001). These actions were taken to build up support and power in these neighbourhoods, but the cartel's leaders, in particular Escobar, had a personal sense of exclusion from elite society in Medellín. By following the same patterns of clientelist politics as the formal politicians and providing security where formal sources had omitted to do so, the cartel was able to establish a substantial and enduring power base. The time when the cartel was gaining economic power coincided with industry losing power. As factories closed and other sources of employment were lost under the pressure of the global recession, the cartel cultivated the disenfranchised youth of Medellín's *barrios* as *sicarios* [young assassins]. Employment by the cartel was seen as a way to achieve riches that would otherwise, in such an unequal city, be completely unavailable.

Escobar and others in the cartel had various formal political successes. Escobar was elected to the House of Representatives in 1982, and many politicians elected that year were funded by 'narco-donations' (Filippone, 1994). Similarly, Medellín Cartel leader Carlos Lehder set up his own political party, the Latin Nationalist Movement, in 1986, despite being a fugitive at the time. However, they were never successful in establishing a permanent foothold in formal politics. Part of the reason behind this was class and status: the elites in Medellín might have succeeded in preventing infiltration by the cartel precisely because they were so exclusive.

Following Escobar's election to the House of Representatives in 1982, the future minister of justice Rodrigo Lara Bonilla, who had lost to Escobar, accused him of being a drug lord on national television. As a result of the ensuing scandal, Escobar resigned, but he had Lara Bonilla assassinated in 1984. To avoid prosecution for trafficking and other offences, and to regain favour in the corridors of formal power, in 1984 Escobar offered to donate US\$3 billion to the national economy, and when that was rejected he offered to pay off the entire national debt of US\$10 billion (Filippone, 1994: 338). This offer, too, was refused, but his political influence penetrated the highest offices, and, offended by the refusal and determined to block the establishment of an extradition treaty with the United States, Escobar declared war on the State. The theatre for this war was not uniquely, but predominantly, Medellín.

The war against the State that Escobar declared in the mid-1980s took the form of a bombing campaign, the assassination of presidential candidates, and a reward of more than US\$2,000 for the killing of any police officer in Medellín (Abadinsky, 2009). At the height of the violence, car

DOI: 10.1057/9781137397362.0007

bombs terrorised the city, partly as an instrument of gang warfare and partly as a weapon of war against the State. A *'plomo o plata'* ['lead or silver' – meaning bullets or money] approach to political influence was adopted. Politicians, ministers, human rights activists, union members, journalists, academics, and police were killed as the cartel, headed by Escobar, marshalled vast swathes of unemployed, disenfranchised youth to his cause and in effect created an army to do his bidding. The *comunas* on the slopes of the city bore the brunt of this violence, but as it escalated, more central areas, including El Poblado, were increasingly affected. The bombing of the Monaco Building in El Poblado in 1988 marked the start of bombing campaigns in more central areas; in the words of one business leader interviewed, 'We realised that the people up there in the *comunas* could kill us all even if they just came down armed with sticks.'[3]

In the ultimate failure of their aspirations to become formal political actors, we can see many of the exclusionary factors that have under-pinned the rise to power of violent actors in Medellín. Cartel leaders were able to take advantage of the limited economic and political insti-tutional development that had been perpetuated by populist politics and clientelism. This allowed them to build up support in the *comunas* that gave them both informal and – when Escobar was elected to the House of Representatives – formal power. Mirroring the politics of patronage to be found in the formal political sphere, they provided social rights, such as the 450 houses in Barrio Pablo Escobar (Lee, 1991), and so gained legitimacy in the eyes of the inhabitants. The exclusion that they were able to exploit was caused by the impenetrable nature of elites in the city. However, this very impenetrability was also arguably what limited Escobar's power.

The acute levels of violence in Medellín are almost synonymous with Pablo Escobar in the popular imagination, but it is important to remem-ber the long-term, deep-rooted causes that gave rise to and facilitated his power. After his death in 1993, the violence did not disappear. The killing of footballer Andres Escobar (no relation to Pablo) after Colombia's disappointing performance in the 1994 World Cup and his disastrous own-goal drew the world's attention to the continuation of the violence in Medellín despite Escobar's death. The inequality, poverty, and exclu-sion that drove the violence were still very much present (Ceballos Melguizo and Cronshaw, 2001). It is argued that after the demise of the cartel, narco-traffic became a more 'horizontal' industry, with multiple small criminal groups rather than large, vertical organisations (Gutiérrez

DOI: 10.1057/9781137397362.0007

and Jaramillo, 2004). What can be seen in the cartel's rise to power is the importance of social and economic exclusion in the *comunas* and clientelism to the way power was established.

Criminal gangs

Many of the violent and other crimes in the *comunas* were perpetrated by criminal gangs. These gangs were not affiliated with the political players – the cartel, the militia, or the paramilitaries – and they made no attempt to enter the para-political arena to provide security or public goods. The delinquency of petty criminals did, however, lend legitimacy to the violence carried out by those armed groups in the name of security.

Criminal gangs have been present in Medellín since the 1960s (Ceballos Melguizo and Cronshaw, 2001). These gangs tended to be associated with smuggling and criminal activities and were the 'heavies' called in to do the dirty work. The workings of these groups have been contrasted with the organised structures of the criminal gangs that arose following the economic recession of the 1980s and the transformative impact of the cartel, the Marxist militias, and the paramilitaries. 'Most dangerous criminals of the era were still picturesque local figures, urban bandits who led criminal actions with several participants' (Ceballos Melguizo and Cronshaw, 2001: 117). This changed in the 1980s when unemployment of up to 60 per cent in the *comunas* (Filippone, 1994) coincided with the rise of narco-traffic, and working in narco-traffic with the charismatic, populist leaders of the cartel brought with it the promise of enormous wealth.

In the 1980s, a distinction developed between the youths who joined with the cartel, militia, or paramilitaries and those who joined street gangs, who were perceived as delinquents who posed a danger to morality, security, and order in the neighbourhoods. These gangs were called *chichipato* gangs, and their criminal activity was put down to their addiction to *bazuco* – a cheap derivative of coca paste used to make cocaine. They were involved in robberies and territorial conflicts, and their 'Dante-esque' delinquency was often the target of the 'cleanings' and impositions of moral order by left-wing militias, right-wing paramilitaries, or the cartel (Filippone, 1994). The youth gangs of the *barrios* were hence a source of violence in two ways: they were themselves perpetrators of violence, and their actions also justified the use of violence by other actors to 'clean' the streets and provide security. Even the drug traffickers could claim that they were working for the good of the city by

DOI: 10.1057/9781137397362.0007

investing in these poorer areas, and they would take pains to point out that they never encouraged drug-use in Medellín itself, nor would they go near the toxic substance *bazuco* (Filippone, 1994).

The criminal gangs, and the disenfranchised youths who tend to populate them, are perpetrators of violence. They have no pretentions, however, to providing security, unlike the cartel, the militia, and the para-militaries. The violence of these delinquents is nowhere near the level of the systematised, political violence perpetrated by the other actors. However, in the popular imagination they are not only the main culprits but also legitimise the other forms of violence, and in effect empower armed groups who claim to provide security.

The urban militia

The urban militias developed their power bases in much the same way as the rural Marxist guerrillas: they claimed to provide security to those whom formal elites, more concerned with maintaining hierarchy and patronage, had systematically excluded, with the aim of establishing themselves as para-State actors. The thoroughgoing dynamics of exclusion, inequality, and lack of security can be seen in the way the militia established their power base. Although ostensibly adopting a politics of supporting the masses against the elite, the militia also had military aims and were themselves perpetrators of violence.

In the mid-1980s, the Marxist guerrilla groups that had been mainly active and concentrated in rural areas expanded their operations into the city. This was a military decision, although urban areas remained peripheral to the general Marxist guerrilla cause. It was also part of the peace agreement between the government and the M19 rebels in 1984 that they would become legitimate political actors and build peace camps in major Colombian cities, including Medellín (Lamb, 2010). The main militia group in Medellín was the Milicia del Pueblo para el Pueblo [Militia of the People, for the People], led by the charismatic Pablo García. Other groups sprang up later – associated with the guerrilla groups M19 and the ELN – following the 'blueprint' established by the Milicia del Pueblo (Gutiérrez and Jaramillo, 2004).

The militia gained power, according to one leader because, 'we do social work by day' and 'military work by night' (Gutiérrez and Jaramillo, 2004: 22). The 'social work' refers to social cleansing of the criminal and delinquent elements in a neighbourhood – including drugs-related gangs. The militia started moving into Medellín in

DOI: 10.1057/9781137397362.0007

Comuna 1, in the northeast of the city. This lower-class neighbourhood had had various problems of exclusion and criminality, and the militia's *modus operandi* of raising revolutionary consciousness and providing security from delinquency was a success. According to militia leaders, they were fulfilling the role of the State, which was consistently found to be complicit with other armed groups, and the militia's actions were popular with the official Juntas de Acción Comunal [Neighbourhood Community Action Groups].

The actions of the militia are a further example of the way that the cycle of violence is perpetuated in Medellín. The fact that the militia found spaces in which their social work could justify their military work was in part a consequence not of the absence of formal powers but of the way that political power and exclusivity was maintained by the city's political elites. This in turn indicates a further problematic political dynamic in Medellín: the proximity of criminal and political violence, embodied by paramilitary groups.

Paramilitaries

Paramilitaries have a long history in Colombia. Their main function officially has been to provide 'security' and combat the guerrilla left, but they have also been involved in various drugs organisations and criminal activities. They started to gain power in Medellín in the mid-1990s. Since their development during La Violencia and during the 1960s, they had focused on the protection of landowners in rural areas from the guerrilla groups. With the formation of the paramilitary groups Muerte a Secuestradores [Death to Kidnappers – MAS] in the 1980s and the Perseguidos por Pablo Escobar [People Persecuted by Pablo Escobar – PePEs] in the 1990s, paramilitaries began to gain power in urban areas. Medellín had particularly strong support for paramilitary groups because of the perceived need for security, particularly during the 1990s, when paramilitaries became responsible for the majority of violence in the city (Issacson, 2014).

Paramilitaries acquired a larger role in Medellín's politics after the death of Pablo Escobar. Throughout their history, paramilitaries have often been seen as a continuation of legitimate force, particularly by formal, more conservative, political actors. Their proximity to legitimate forces is argued to be an irresponsible blurring of the lines between politics, legitimacy, and criminality. Their role in the levels of violence in Colombia is one of the most controversial questions in contemporary

DOI: 10.1057/9781137397362.0007

Colombian politics, with some seeing them as a source of violence, and others seeing them as a source of security.

The line between paramilitary and military activities has been – and, many argue, continues to be – blurred (Filippone, 1994; Gutiérrez and Jaramillo, 2004; BBC, 2013). In some cases this blurring has been explicit, as in the legitimisation of paramilitary groups as private security forces. In other cases, paramilitaries have allegedly been involved in operations to pacify areas on behalf of the State, expropriate land for multinationals, and perform the notorious 'cleansings' to quell delinquency in crime-ridden neighbourhoods (Amnesty International, 2005; Avilés, 2006; Taussig, 2005). The most recent spike in violence has been put down to the fragmentation of the drugs trade, and paramilitary involvement in associated criminal gangs, known locally as *bacrims* (BBC, 2013).

The State

Unclear lines between legitimate State actors and other forces, particularly when they have been united in opposition to the guerrilla groups and militia, are a feature of the city's history. Bribery and other forms of illegitimate political influence have been rife, and State actors, including the police, lack the trust of the communities. The clientelist policies adopted by all actors, including the State, have exacerbated the difficulties in distinguishing between legitimate and illegitimate powers. The State's attempts to quell the violence with accords and peace talks with informal political actors indicates how complex these relationships have been.

The drug cartel and its leaders, despite their political aspirations, were considered beyond the pale of possible formal political alliances, although there were many informal ones. They were hugely influential because of their enormous wealth, and the State was forced into a compromise with the Medellín Cartel and Pablo Escobar. In response to demands and threats from 'The Extraditables', a group founded by Escobar and other drug traffickers, the Colombian Constitution of 1991 initially banned the extradition of Colombian citizens. In return, Escobar agreed to be confined to his luxury custom-built jail 'La Catedral' [The Cathedral], situated on land which he had sold to the State.

At this point Escobar had many enemies, including the Cali Cartel, which, along with Escobar's former colleagues the Castaño brothers, had set up the paramilitary group the PePEs. When Escobar 'escaped' his own prison, numerous parties put up funds for a reward for his capture, and

DOI: 10.1057/9781137397362.0007

international governments donated equipment and expertise that would eventually lead to his capture and death at the hands of the National Police in December 1993. Although State forces did eventually kill Pablo Escobar, this was possible because he had lost his strategic alliances with other groups and because the Colombian State had gained international support.

In contrast, para-State and paramilitary groups were recognised as having legitimacy in the *comunas*, and a political solution that recognised the bases of their power was deemed necessary in the early 1990s (Boudon, 1996). The formal political powers offered to recognise the militia and the paramilitaries by legitimising their security role. Whilst this was a recognition of the political processes behind the violence, it also exacerbated the lack of a clear distinction between legitimate and illegitimate force, continuing some of the political underpinnings of the violence.

In 1991, the municipality of Medellín, with backing from the national government, entered into peace talks with the militia. The national government had sent resources to support this process after receiving a request from the mayor of Medellín for assistance in dealing with the 'communist' threat. The arrangement was that former militia would come together to maintain security in the neighbourhood, but in a formalised way. The resulting organisation was called the Cooperativa de Vigilancia y Servicio a la Comunidad [the Surveillance and Community Service Cooperative – COOSERCOM], and it involved some 800 militia members being officially responsible for security in their neighbourhoods. It is widely held that this initiative failed owing to the disintegration of the militia and the proximity of COOSERCOM to criminal activity.

In 1994, paramilitarism was legalised, using the legislation passed in the 1960s that allowed civilians to take up arms and be trained by the military for their own defence (Amnesty International, 2005). Paramilitary groups, formally known as Servicios Especiales de Vigilancia y Seguridad Privada [Special Vigilance and Private Security Services], acquired the epithet 'Las Convivir' [Live Together] and functioned as legitimate private security forces that could be contracted by vulnerable neighbourhoods, businesses, or landowners. The formation of these groups was strongly criticised by liberal forces in Medellín and human rights organisations internationally, but they received robust support in the *comunas* of Medellín, where the violence at this point was at its peak.

DOI: 10.1057/9781137397362.0007

2008, Colombia's Constitutional Court acknowledged that in the overwhelming majority of cases of sexual violence reported, the perpetrator was a member of one of Colombia's illegal armed groups, or 'in some isolated cases ... the Armed Forces', and furthermore that these actions were carried out with impunity. As such, the Court recognised that 'sexual violence against women is a habitual, extended, systematic, and invisible practice in the context of the Colombian Armed Conflict' and went on to clarify that

> these hundreds of atrocious acts ... in themselves constitute serious crimes under national legislation and International Humanitarian Law, and ... together appear before this Court to be a factual picture of violence, cruelty, and barbarism on which has been placed a cloak of almost total invisibility, silence, and impunity, both at the official and extra-official level. (Corte Constitucional de Colombia, Auto 092/08, author's translation)[5]

Amnesty International has reported that illegal armed groups use threats and acts of sexual violence 'to control the behaviour of women, both civilians and their own combatants, including through rape and forced contraception, pregnancy, and abortion' (Amnesty International, 2011: 15).

Conflict-related sexual violence is enabled by a context in which rates of gender-based violence and violence against women are exceptionally high. Statistics on this are very hard to assemble, but the most comprehensive data set available in Colombia is based on medical examinations, and the rate is thought to be drastically underestimated (Amnesty International, 2011). In 2010, the rate of sexual violence was at its highest for 10 years, at 49 per 100,000 population (Human Rights Watch, 2011: 25). Displaced women have been found to be particularly vulnerable to violence and face overwhelming barriers to accessing justice or related health care (Human Rights Watch, 2011). In Medellín, gender-disaggregated data on the various indicators of violence are not available, but reports from women's rights groups indicate that violence is particularly high in the *barrios*.

Gendered ideas of power and leadership, of who can acquire power and what can be done to maintain it, are permeated by imagery and values recreated in Colombia's long-running conflicts. In the words of one city councillor,

> This is *tumbao* culture. *Tumbao* means that I've toppled you, I win, I'm the most important, and if you don't know that it was me that did it, even better. ... He is the man, that's how Pablo worked. That's how he got what he got,

because he was determined to beat everyone else. *Ese es el macho, ese es Pablo Escobar.*[6]

The culture of leadership among political and business leaders was also referred to as *tumbao*, which is difficult to translate. A related meaning of the word comes from its origins as a Caribbean dance, and it can refer to a particularly confident way of walking – a 'swagger' or a 'strut' for men, and a certain 'sway' for women. At the same time, *tumbao* can mean a con, or even a robbery, and it is also related to the Spanish verb *tumbar*, which means to overthrow or knock out. It is associated with another leadership value – being *vivo* – which means being smart, even crafty, and taking advantage of people, preferably without them knowing. The importance of this aspect of the culture is frequently stressed in the way people involved in Medellín's transformation explain the violence, and the senses of identity and power which are associated with violence, at both the everyday level and the political level.

A strong trope within elite cultures in Medellín is that the breakdown of family values was one cause of the rise of violence:

> We've gone from having children who were raised by their mothers a few years ago to children growing up in a family crisis. That is, the family is no longer a nuclear family underpinned by values and cultural identity. Today children are brought up by institutions and the media – by nannies, by aunts. … The woman has changed her role, and with this change in role, the woman is no longer the mother who takes responsibility for bringing up and educating the children which she was in another time. … I think that the change of model [of the family] has something to do with the fact that our values and identity have strongly changed.[7]

This diagnosis, commonly heard and often accepted by working women themselves, resonates with explanations of violence as a breakdown of social order that justifies a reinforcement of traditional values. Another strand of thought, however, is that narco-traffic took off in Antioquia *because* of the region's traditional values, which include productivity and savings, and also the value of being *vivo*, which is considered typical of Antioquia. Antioquia prides itself on being Colombia's most entrepreneurial region: 'Our people are our best export. There are Antioqueños everywhere. We have an Antioqueño in the desert renting out camels,'[8] said the head of one of the city's prominent business organisations. There is also the often quoted injunction 'Get money, my son. Get it honourably, but if you can't get it honourably, get it anyway,' which has been

DOI: 10.1057/9781137397362.0007

used as an explanation, along with consumer culture, for why so many people seemed willing to take advantages of the riches on offer from involvement with narco-traffic, regardless of any ethical concerns. 'In this sense,' said a sociologist who had been involved in the political party Compromiso Ciudadano, 'elite culture and the culture of narco-traffic were both typical Antioquian cultures.'[9]

Conclusion

There is a geography to Medellín's violence. Whilst the city does exhibit the characteristics most associated with urban violence, an exploration of the political, economic, and social context shows how these structural factors are only part of the explanation of how violence became endemic. The city's inequality and lack of security, and the political and economic disenfranchisement in its communities, have been a source of power for drug traffickers, militia, and paramilitary actors. Associations between the State and other actors created a sense of exclusion that the militias addressed with their 'social work' of raising revolutionary consciousness, the drug lords addressed by providing employment and the hope of riches, and the paramilitaries addressed by offering 'security'. Inequality and economic exclusion, when coupled with the potential riches on offer through narco-traffic and involvement with the cartel and the competitive, entrepreneurial tropes of power and leadership in Antioquia, can be understood as a motive for disenfranchised youth to become Escobar's *sicarios*, and for other, ostensibly more legitimate, actors to be complicit.

Medellín's crisis of violence can hence be understood as a problem of the formation of political processes and political space. To understand the political spaces – the *comunas* – over which violent groups were able to establish power involves an understanding of the range of violent political processes at work, from the legacy of Colombia's political conflict to the cultural tropes of power, masculinity, and leadership that frame interpretations of situations in such a way that violence seems justified to its perpetrators. In this sense, the geographical solutions to Medellín's problems – the infrastructure and transport projects that have become known as social urbanism – seem appropriate. The chapters that follow explore these policies in terms of their interaction with the construction of political space in Medellín. Whilst the Metrocable, libraries, and public spaces can be seen as addressing the inequality and exclusion that

DOI: 10.1057/9781137397362.0007

'changed the skin of the city', they can also be seen as reinforcing elite power, in a way that may compound as much as challenge the political, social, and economic dynamics that underpinned the widespread violence.

Notes

1   'Enroque paisa' is literally translated as 'Antioquian castling', referring to the defensive move in the game of chess. 'Paisa' is the colloquial name for an inhabitant of Antioquia.

2   Focus group of business leaders, 25 July 2012.

3   Focus group of business leaders, 25 July 2012.

4   Business leader, interview, 8 August 2012.

5   Available at: http://www.corteconstitucional.gov.co/relatoria/autos/2008/a092-08.htm

6   Medellín councillor, interview, 16 July 2012.

7   Focus group of business leaders, 25 July 2012.

8   Business leader, interview, 8 August 2012.

9   Academic and NGO activist, interview, 7 August 2012.

DOI: 10.1057/9781137397362.0007

3
The Miracle? Social Urbanism

Abstract: *This chapter places social urbanism in a global context by examining the policies associated with the 'Medellín Miracle' alongside urban regeneration interventions from other 'model cities', including most notably Barcelona. City branding has become a global business as cities compete for foreign investment and various 'mega-events' such as the Olympics. Policies to achieve model city status tend to include the types of project that have been central to social urbanism: mass transport systems, public space, public art, and iconic buildings. Medellín is, however, exceptional in that these policies were designed, promoted, and enacted in a context of extreme violence, inequality, exclusion, and informality. The argument here is that the relationship between urban regeneration policies and violence needs to be understood in terms of whether the power struggles underpinning violence in the city have changed.*

Keywords: Barcelona model; model cities; urban regeneration; urban violence

Maclean, Kate. *Social Urbanism and the Politics of Violence: The Medellín Miracle*. Basingstoke: Palgrave Macmillan, 2015. DOI: 10.1057/9781137397362.0008.

Medellín's Miracle has generated headlines worldwide. Some coverage in media, literary, and policy circles has oversimplified the transition, proclaiming that the city is now 'safe' and implying that this miraculous transformation was directly due to the impact of the architectural and infrastructural projects implemented. The *New York Times* published various claims that crime had been successfully fought with architecture (*New York Times*, 2012). The BBC praised the city's 'remarkable renewal' (BBC, 2010), which has been favourably contrasted with the attempts at urban regeneration of its rival city Bogotá (*The Guardian*, 2012) and was described by the *Washington Post* as a remarkable transition from 'drugs violence to tourist destination' (*Washington Post*, 2010). The Medellín Miracle has taken place in the context of a broader 'rebranding' of Colombia (Echeverri et al., 2010), and against the background of a concerted effort by the country's literary figures to reinforce an external perception of Colombia's cultural richness and overcome what for many in the West is an automatic association with narco-traffic (LaRosa and Mejía, 2012).

Over the period in question, Medellín has not been the only 'model city' of urban regeneration. Urban planning praxis has globalised over the last 20 years (Robinson, 2006), and Medellín's success comes after similar transformative stories from Barcelona, Bilbao, Curitiba, and Rotterdam (González, 2011). The 'Medellín model', which policymakers from other violence-affected cities in Mexico, South Africa, and Brazil are keen to replicate, explicitly derives from and bears much similarity to the approaches of its model city predecessors. Iconic architecture projects, infrastructural investment, and high-profile cultural events have become a planning manual for any city with an eye on the global stage. Although claims are often made about the regenerative potential of such policies, they have been consistently criticised for aiming to attract international investment from tourists, multinationals, or the 'transnational capitalist class', at the expense of inclusion, equality, and any sense of a 'right to the city' (Sklair, 2010).

Despite many similarities between social urbanism and the policies implemented by other model cities, Medellín's experiences are unique. The replication of these policies in the context of extreme urban violence and their apparent success in reducing violence have stimulated interest in Medellín, but the high profile of the city's regeneration is also the result of concerted efforts to improve the image of the city and attract foreign direct investment. Whilst the neoliberal project underpinning

DOI: 10.1057/9781137397362.0008

urban regeneration in the North has been associated with increased informality, a reduction in welfare, and gentrification (Lees et al., 2010), the political landscape in Latin America in the twenty-first century presents different challenges. The present exploration of Medellín's urban regeneration aims to critique Western urban theory, which tends to have pretensions to be 'global' (Robinson, 2006). Nevertheless, the powerful critiques that have been marshalled against formulaic model urbanism in the North – most prominently charges that it results in displacement, gentrification, and elite revanchism – are pertinent to the Medellín example, as they highlight the crucial question of how power has changed in the city. Although, if some headlines are to be believed, libraries and metro trains can be used to address urban violence, those who were involved in developing and implementing the policies behind Medellín's Miracle are very clear that this dramatic transformation has been a long-term political process.

This chapter reviews the policies that came to be known as 'social urbanism'. From the mid-1990s, the argument that the root cause of the violence was a 'historical social debt' owed to marginalised areas of the city by ruling elites became a dominant narrative. To tackle this geographical marginalisation, policies were developed and promoted explicitly to 'change the skin of the city' – a phrase that recalls Barcelona's 'urban acupuncture' (Blanco et al., 2011). Interventions addressed mobility, infrastructure, and the provision of public parks and spaces, and were aimed at encouraging responsible political participation and socioeconomic development from below. One prominent example is the innovative Metrocable, the world's first use of Alpine cable-car technology in urban public transportation, which connects the exclusive southern neighbourhood of El Poblado with two of the most stigmatised areas of the city. In another high-profile example, five library parks have been constructed in the poorest areas of the city. These dramatic buildings were the result of international architectural competitions and are a conspicuous demonstration of the commitment to invest in the poorest areas. In many ways, these policies were inspired by international models – including Catalan schools of architecture, Brazilian models of participatory politics and socioeconomic development, northern Italian models of inclusive economy and cooperatives, and Richard Florida's work on the promotion of creative industries. Although critiques of these models are centred on the global North, the typical characteristics of cities in the

DOI: 10.1057/9781137397362.0008

global South – informality, exclusion, lack of infrastructure, transition to democracy – pose particular challenges to the ways in which models of urban regeneration are developed and analysed. In this chapter, I outline the policies that have travelled to Medellín and how they are grounded in the particular political context of that city. I also look at the way issues associated with underdevelopment and urban violence have shaped the Medellín model.

Medellín and the model city

The Medellín Miracle is an example of the globalisation of urban planning (Robinson, 2006; McCann and Ward, 2011), and Medellín is one of many model cities to have emerged since the 1990s. Urban policies pioneered, or implemented with particular success, in Barcelona, Bilbao, Paris, Rotterdam, San Francisco, and Vancouver, among many other cities, have made their way around the world via circuits of experts, trade fairs, league tables, and mega-events to create a global industry in urban policy (Ward, 2006; González, 2011). Many of these cities are in the global North, and many are 'second-tier' cities, vying to compete with established capitals and financial centres (McCann and Ward, 2011). These models have been criticised for representing a neoliberal agenda in which urban policy is designed to attract foreign direct investment from a transnational capitalist class rather than to develop a 'right to the city' for all its citizens (Lees et al., 2010; Sklair, 2010). Policies which have improved a city's economic indicators are argued also to have gentrified neighbourhoods, displaced working-class populations, and increased urban inequality. However, there is also a participatory element to these models which, although it may resonate with the neoliberal agenda in terms of communitarian ideals of a small State, can also open up political spaces for progressive interventions.

Despite each model city being championed for its innovation, a particular palette of policies has come to define prize-winning urban regeneration. Mass transport systems, public spaces, and iconic architecture projects have all featured, in different ways, in the cities mentioned above. Sustainability, in terms of both finance and the environment, entrepreneurialism, and the promotion of cultural industries are also hallmarks of model cities. Barcelona became known for its urban

DOI: 10.1057/9781137397362.0008

renewal projects in the run-up to the Olympics in 1992; there were major improvements in infrastructure, including the airport, and 'eye-pleasing' public areas were developed to attract investment to otherwise marginalised areas (Monclús, 2003). Similarly, the iconic architectural projects of Bilbao and the urban sustainability of Vancouver have been reference points for discussions of urban renewal in cities as diverse as Dubai, Buenos Aires, and Plymouth. The effects of these policies have been debated, but there is no doubt that they have been influential, through various networks, flows, and practices, in cities around the world (Peck and Theodore, 2010).

With the emergence of the phenomenon of 'city branding' as part of the neoliberal project to attract foreign direct investment, including in the form of tourism, these policy recommendations have also been followed in the South (Robinson, 2006). City branding can be distinguished from 'city marketing' by the use of branding techniques to promote a city on the world stage, rather than responding to market needs or referring solely to economic production (Kavaratzis, 2004). City branding has been related to Olympic campaigns and the tourism industry, and it includes policies to promote cities' cultural and artistic heritage whilst remaining within a market model. City league tables, measuring everything from the safest city to the greenest, also facilitate the emergence of a global marketplace not only for cities but also for urban policy and planning (Burrows et al., 2005).

The migration of these policies has been anything but linear. Contrary to the idea that best practice is 'transferred' from one city to another as a technical innovation, the politics of how city models influence policy is 'messy' (Larner and Laurie, 2010). The way that cities take up certain policies or interventions is as much a function of their respective political situations, and their specific regeneration agendas, as it is a question of whether or not a policy represents best practice (Crot, 2010). Hence, although the urban regeneration policies represented by model cities tend to be thought of as transferable 'technical' fixes, their effectiveness and influence need to be analysed within the local political, economic, and social context.

There is a post-colonial politics to the 'flows of knowledge, expertise, technologies and cosmopolitan policy actors' (Peck and Theodore, 2010: 171) that underpin the mobility of policies, as Northern knowledge is recognised as 'expertise' and Northern cities tend to host elite educational institutions. The city league tables developed by various

DOI: 10.1057/9781137397362.0008

media and policy groups tend to speak to the preferences of capital and enterprise in the global North, and global cultural and sporting events have a pronounced colonial legacy. The tastes underlying the beautifying of public spaces have colonial inflections, and this beautification of cities can be seen as part of the marginalisation of working classes in the post-industrial word (Robinson, 2006). The inequalities of the outsourcing of manufacturing jobs, gentrification, and the dominance of 'global cities' have been the focus of 'theoretical' discussions of urbanism, which tend to reference case studies in Europe and North America yet claim to refer to 'The City' in general (Lees, 2012). The specificities of city case studies – their particular political, economic, and cultural fabrics, identities, and articulations – need to be the basis of theorisations of how policy develops, without losing sight of theoretical insights from elsewhere.

Whilst the majority of model cities are in the global North, a number of cities in the South have been influential in global understandings of urban development. Brazil has led the way, with Curitiba becoming a reference point for ecological development (Irazábal, 2005) and Porto Alegre for participatory democracy (Crot, 2010; De Sousa Santos, 1998). The Medellín Miracle itself has become another such city branding export. Most associated with the Medellín model is the principle of using policies of socioeconomic development to reduce violence. Particular interest in this principle has been shown in Mexico, which is the latest place in which the atrocious effects of narco-related violence have erupted. The technical intervention most associated with Medellín is the Metrocable. Cities as diverse as London and La Paz have built cable-cars as part of their public transport system, with an eye to the innovation from Medellín.

In analysing social urbanism and the technical interventions that are associated with the Medellín Miracle, I want to situate the Medellín model within the comparative context of other models of urban regeneration from around the world and debates about city branding. The most interesting thing about the Medellín Miracle is that although it recreates policies that are in general familiar to urban development specialists, it does so in a context of extreme violence – apparently with some success. But it is impossible to qualify or assess the apparent positive impacts of social urbanism without understanding the politics behind these policies and seeing the miracle as an ongoing, contextualised process.

DOI: 10.1057/9781137397362.0008

The Medellín Miracle: the policies

The policies that made the miracle have a history, and some were planned since the 1960s. However, they began to come to fruition in the mid-1990s, after which they gained momentum and, under the administration of Mayor Sergio Fajardo, became known under the umbrella term 'social urbanism'. The policies of social urbanism had in common a mission to reverse the historical social debt that the city's elites owed to neglected areas, especially the hillside *comunas* of Medellín, and to change the skin of the city by addressing the spatialised exclusion that so graphically characterised the city's inequality (Echeverri and Orsini, 2012). The policies implemented under social urbanism were explicitly inspired by the Barcelona model (Brand, 2013). However, the claims made about Medellín's social urbanism, in the context of extreme, endemic violence, are very different from those made for model cities in other parts of the world, and they cast the politics of urban planning in a new light. Given the violence and its relationship with the urban environment, the Medellín model may go some way to address the structural inequalities that underpin the violence. However, whilst changing the skin is indeed important, questions have been raised about the extent to which the changes are merely cosmetic (Hylton, 2007), and whether they reinforce rather than challenge the inequality, exclusion, and power struggles that, for many, are the basis of Medellín's violence.

Infrastructure projects

Big infrastructure projects are a feature of cities undergoing transformation, and also a feature of rebranding (Currid and Williams, 2010; Pratt, 2011). However, they are also a modernisation project – particularly in the context of the global South – and aim to build up cities so that they can participate in the global market (Watson, 2009). In the context of Medellín, these big infrastructure projects have taken on a particular meaning in the context of the battle against violence and the recognition of the city's social debt to the poor. The iconic infrastructure projects are central to the aims of changing mobility around the city and addressing the inequality and exclusion which were recognised as causing the violence. These projects also coincide with urban interventions that had become, by the twenty-first century, familiar to urbanists.

DOI: 10.1057/9781137397362.0008

The most iconic elements of social urbanism are the transport projects, including most notably the Metrocable, which extended the terrestrial metro. These projects were designed to address the way in which the city's infrastructure had developed to favour the priorities, patterns of mobility, and aesthetic vision of the elites. The metro and Metrocable were intended to change mobility around the city and construct a more inclusive economy, as people on the periphery would be able to access wealthier markets in the centre. There is also an important political, symbolic element to such investments in poorer, stigmatised areas: the metro and the Metrocable are signs of conspicuous investment in previously neglected and stigmatised areas (Brand and Dávila, 2011). Particularly in the Latin American context, public investment in transport infrastructure is a marked change in direction from the structural adjustment policies of the 1980s that saw many such systems closed. The oft-quoted phrase from Enrique Peñalosa, the mayor of Bogotá who oversaw that city's Bus Transit System – 'A developed country is not a place where the poor have cars; it's where the rich use public transportation'¹ – is indicative of the change in the definition of development that came not only from civic protests but also from a recognition that the continent needed to boost consumption.

Although its development predated the social urbanism policies that the city has become known for, the Medellín metro indicates the trajectory that urban planning was taking and the conditions of possibility of the evolving political climate. The metro was completed in the early 1990s, when, as will be discussed in more detail in the next chapter, there was a concerted effort at the national level to invest in Medellín and deal with the crisis of violence. At the global level, there was an enthusiasm for mass public transit systems, despite the fact that they are rarely profit making and require subsidies (Gilbert, 2008). This followed successful transport projects in Barcelona in the run-up to the Olympics, as well as in Curitiba, which has a mass transit bus system that is renowned as an example of inclusive, environmentally sustainable city transport (Lindau et al., 2010). In developing countries, which tend to be characterised by exceptionally high volumes of traffic and informal, inefficient transport systems, mass transit was posited as a solution not only in terms of urban design but also in terms of indirect efficiency benefits and the ability to attract foreign direct investment (Fouracre et al., 2003).

The metro was originally planned in 1968, and foreign financing was sought, but repeatedly turned down on the ground that the project was

DOI: 10.1057/9781137397362.0008

not feasible (Echavarría et al., 2002). Medellín's metro eventually received approval in the early 1980s under President Betancur, who was originally from Antioquia, despite continued concerns about the project's feasibility. Finally completed in 1994, the Medellín metro project had cost almost US$2 billion, and the foreign debts that had funded it could not be serviced. In a scathing review of the project by the Inter-American Development Bank (IADB), the metro is held up as an example of bad management practice leading to the need for a bail-out (Echavarría et al., 2002). Nevertheless, people in Medellín deem the metro to be a success. It is often heard that Medellín has 'the best metro in the world', and citizens are particularly proud of the 'metro culture', a widely publicised campaign encouraging good behaviour on the metro, which is claimed to have been so successful that minimal policing is needed within the metro itself.

The 'jewel in the crown' (Brand, 2013) of Medellín's social urbanism is the Metrocable. The Metrocable links the metro system, which owing to the city's topography runs only the length of the valley (Gilbert, 2008), with two of the most notorious neighbourhoods – San Domingo and San Javier – as it navigates the steep Andean hillsides that surround the city. It hence connects the poorest, most stigmatised neighbourhoods with the city centre, drastically cutting journey time between those areas and allowing people living on the hillsides to travel more easily to work and to the markets in the centre. Although the direct impacts of the Metrocable are debatable – it has been found, for example, that it is regularly used by only 10 per cent of residents of San Javier and Santo Domingo (Brand and Dávila, 2011) – it is internationally recognised not only for the feat of engineering which it required but as a symbol of investment in the poorest areas of the city. It has encouraged those from richer neighbourhoods to take the picturesque journey over the hilltops, and so witness, albeit at a distance, the neighbourhoods that they know only as stigmatised battlegrounds on the television news. A ride on the Metrocable is one of the main parts of the tour that official visitors to the city – including Condoleezza Rice – are taken on, and it has resulted in a number of very positive reports (e.g. BBC, 2010; *Guardian*, 2014; *New York Times*, 2012; *Washington Post*, 2010).

The Metrocable was made possible in part by the popularity of the metro, and the consistency with which public transport reforms were seen to be part of the palette of urban planning policies recreated in model cities around the globe (Fouracre et al., 2003). The Metrocable

DOI: 10.1057/9781137397362.0008

lines were not isolated investments; they were part of a participatory process known as a Proyecto Urbano Integral [Integrated Urban Upgrading Programme – PUI], which emphasised the importance of community participation at every stage (Blanco and Kobayashi, 2009). PUIs were part of a new, integrated approach to urban development in Medellín that started in the 1990s and was known as the Programa Integral de Mejoramiento de Barrios Subnormales [Integrated Slum Upgrading Programme – PRIMED]. PRIMED, which is often compared to Rio's Favela–Bairro [Slum to Neighbourhood] programme, focused on community participation as well as the upgrading of public services (Samper, 2012). In addition to its economic impacts and political symbolism, this change in political process is central to understanding Medellín's transformation and the relationship between the city's social urbanism and violence.

Iconic architecture

From the Sydney Opera House to Bilbao's Guggenheim Museum, 'iconic' architecture has become a central feature of urban regeneration projects. The model cities that have become global reference points for urban regeneration are branded by such iconic structures, commissioned as part of the regeneration process and executed by 'star' architects (Sklair, 2010). In a sense, this is not new, as cities have been defined by prominent architectural achievements for millennia, but the late twentieth century saw a proliferation of iconic buildings. This was due in part to advances in computer technology, and in part to the role of such monuments in attracting investment, as evidenced by their effectiveness in prominent model cities.

However, as with the monuments that came to define ancient cities, the politics of more modern times can be read in a model city's iconic architecture. The iconic designs of the late twentieth century have been described as monuments to capitalism and consumerism that house financial institutions and shopping malls. Despite being a welcome recognition of the importance of the identity of place in the context of a rapidly globalising world, the aesthetics of such buildings, from Tom Wright's Burj Al Arab in Dubai to the Petronas Towers in Kuala Lumpur, speak more to the esoteric tastes of the 'starchitects', transnational capitalist class, and local elites than to those of the people who inhabit these places on a daily basis (Sklair, 2010).

DOI: 10.1057/9781137397362.0008

The iconic architecture of Medellín can be seen as a continuation of the late twentieth-century trend for regenerating, soon-to-be-model cities to have a definitive architectural triumph (Hylton, 2007). However, as has been observed in other cities following the same trajectory (Monclús, 2003; Crot, 2010), an understanding of the political discourses surrounding these buildings allows a more nuanced analysis of the spaces they create. In Medellín, the rationale behind prominent architecture projects was, in the words of Sergio Fajardo,

> the most beautiful for the most humble, so that the public pride can illuminate us all. The beauty of the architecture is essential: where once there was death, fear, misunderstanding, today we have the most impressive buildings of the highest quality so that we can all find ourselves surrounded by culture, education and peaceful coexistence. (Barcelona Metropolis, 2010)

Placing the highest quality, most beautiful buildings in the poorest areas was part of the commitment to address the historical social debt owed by the city's elites to the poorer areas of the city (*Guardian*, 2012). The decision of which areas constituted 'the poorest' was made on the basis of statistical indicators, rather than patronage, and was part of broader PUI projects which involved community participation (Hernandez García, 2013).

Rather than 'cathedrals of consumption' (Sklair, 2010: 140), the iconic architecture in Medellín has taken the form of 'library parks', which, according to the City's Development Plan for 2004–2007, are intended to 'strengthen the libraries as integral centres for development and culture' (Fajardo Valderrama, 2004: 33). They function as libraries, community and training centres, and crèches. They represent conspicuous investment and are intended to contribute to a more inclusive economy, as they address not only educational needs but also the information gaps that can impede access to available resources.

The most prominent of the library parks is the Biblioteca de los Reyes de España [The Library of the King and Queen of Spain], which consists of three large cube-like structures on the hillside designed to fit in with the surrounding mountainous rocks. The architects were chosen after a competitive international process (*Guardian*, 2012). However, the library parks are not uncontroversial. One comment frequently heard is that they are 'just blocks of concrete' and that although they are symbolically significant, they fail to address the root causes of exclusion in the city. Whilst some deem it a triumph that poorer neighbourhoods and

DOI: 10.1057/9781137397362.0008

informal settlements have been given such a prominent part in the city's rebranding (e.g. Hernandez-García, 2013), others are more sceptical about the levels of significant participation by communities in the design and implementation of these projects, alleging that they glorify the architects and the funders more than the people of the communities themselves. The architects have won prizes, but as one Medellín academic noted with regard to the Biblioteca de los Reyes de España, 'Why on Earth is it named after the king and queen of Spain if it's all meant to be about community and bottom-up development?'[2]

It is characteristic of the policies that made the Medellín Miracle that there is a coincidence between the agenda for inclusion and social development and the needs of the city to attract capital. The library parks fulfil both agendas by creating new spaces that address exclusion in the city through an investment in education and human capital that can contribute to economic development and change the image of the city on the global stage. These aims are not necessarily in contradiction, as social exclusion, particularly when it is associated with the levels of violence observed in Medellín, undermines a city's ability to attract investment. However, as Lefebvre warned, 'monumental buildings [can be used] to mask the will to power and the arbitrariness of power beneath signs and surfaces which claim to express collective will and collective thought' (cited in Sharp et al., 2005: 1002).

Public spaces

Public spaces have historically been an important feature of a city, in terms of both physical infrastructure – the parks, squares, and plazas – and the civic life of the city. Walking in the park, participating in town hall meetings, and even taking public transport are activities accessible to all, and as such these spaces can engender a common identity that is at the core of citizenship. Moreover, the presence of such spaces can stimulate more inclusive political debate and attenuate the potential for the ghettoisation of a city, where spaces become bound by identities and ideas of belonging that can underpin conflict, as the example of Medellín has graphically shown.

The creation of public spaces hence requires more than the construction of physical infrastructure. Public space is inherently social and is defined as much by the way that people interact, converse, and identify with each other within it as by the physical boundaries demarcating the area. In addition to the formal examples given above, more informal

DOI: 10.1057/9781137397362.0008

spaces, such as coffee houses (Sennett, 1977), streets (Atkinson, 2003), and even, in the case of Rio, the beach (Freeman, 2008), can all be deemed 'public'. What all these spaces have in common is that there are no formal barriers to access, but the informal social barriers, in terms of who you know, dress, or etiquette, can be equally powerful.

The development of public spaces, including parks and public art works, has become a familiar feature to urbanists studying regeneration in the context of cities vying for global attention. The Barcelona model is a reference point, as the development of public spaces in marginalised areas, building on the city's rich artistic and architectural heritage, was prominent in its regeneration strategies during the 1980s and 1990s. The importance of public parks, art works, and gardens in urban regeneration, in terms both of attracting investment and tourism and of bolstering citizens' inclusion and sense of belonging, has been exported to cities around the world, with varying degrees of success. Whilst it is argued that the politics behind Barcelona's participatory approach to urban regeneration, following years of repression under Franco, was the key to its success (Crot, 2010), the creation of 'beautiful' public spaces has become a technical element of Barcelona-inspired approaches to urban regeneration. Rather than promoting a right to the city, public spaces have become tools with which to spruce up the neighbourhood and attract wealthier residents, often without reference to the displacement effects that such gentrification can have (Lees, 1998).

Investment in public space and public art has been associated with the potential to promote a sense of identity and place, bolster civic pride, and address social exclusion (Hall and Robertson, 2001), but there is also concern about the effects that such a strategy can produce when it is coupled with the aim of promoting economic development and investment. For instance, Glasgow, a city whose regeneration campaign 'Glasgow's Miles Better' has itself become a point of reference, used urban parks in its culture-led regeneration strategies. These parks had the dual aim of improving the standard of living of the city's residents and making the city more attractive to investors. Although the strategy was promoted as a win–win for residents and investors, 'the underlying social context and local public space needs were undermined by wider economic goals' (Inroy, 2000), as public spaces became privatised, rents increased, and social histories were erased in favour of a more palatable cultural heritage (Sharp et al., 2005).

DOI: 10.1057/9781137397362.0008

Public art, which is intended by definition to 'engage with its audiences and create spaces … within which people can identify themselves' (Sharp et al., 2005: 1003–1004), has, following the Barcelona model, been key to the development of public spaces in the context of late twentieth-century urban regeneration. Prominent public art projects, such as Anthony Gormley's Angel of the North in Gateshead and Anish Kapoor's 'Cloud Gate' in Chicago's AT&T Millennium Park, have had a role in effecting a shift from the 'post-industrial to the cultural city' (Sharp et al., 2005). Public art does, of course, have a long and controversial history as part of the creation and design of cities and ideas of public space. From the Renaissance to the nineteenth century's 'City Beautiful' projects, public art has divided opinion over whether it represents elite/bourgeois revanchism or a celebration of citizens' diversity and creativity (MacLeod, 2002; Smith, 2002, 2012; Slater, 2004).[3]

The lack of public space in Medellín in the 1980s and 1990s was conspicuous. More affluent areas were highly securitised, and the poorer areas on the hillsides, dominated by informal settlements, did not have the luxury of planned parks, squares, or community centres. In 2005, the amount of public space in Medellín was 4.01 square metres per person, which was short of Bogotá's 6 square metres per person, and compared extremely unfavourably with cities known for their public spaces – Buenos Aires (22 square metres per person) and London and New York (both with 20 square metres per person) (Lopez and Kuc, 2009). The lack of public spaces was viewed not only as a symptom of the violence but also as a cause: the spatial exclusion that had resulted from decades of high levels of migration that had not been accommodated by city planners lay behind the economic and social exclusion which had led to such high levels of violence.

According to Medellín's architects, the libraries, parks, and educational institutions that formed the city's new public spaces were intended to be 'spaces of encounter that serve as urban landmarks and gathering spaces for the community' (Castro and Echeverri, 2011: 100). Among the most notable of these interventions are the Botanical Gardens, on 40 acres of land in the centre of the city, which house tropical plants and trees and an aviary and runs academic training programmes and workshops. There had been a Botanical Garden there since the 1800s, but it became a neglected no-go area in the late twentieth century. It was renovated in 2005 and is now part of an extensive area in the centre of the city that also includes a science park (the Parque Explorador), a planetarium,

DOI: 10.1057/9781137397362.0008

and an open park with fountains (the Parque de los Deseos). The Parque Botero, dedicated to one of Colombia's most famous sculptors, Fernando Botero, is also located in the city centre.

Alongside these conspicuous investments, the approach to urban planning in general was explicitly guided by the need to create public space. The PUIs which targeted the most vulnerable neighbourhoods, included the creation and beautification of community spaces by building walk ways and escalators, pedestrianising certain areas, greening the streets, and increasing the area of public space per person (Castro and Echeverri, 2011). The PUIs also include the enhanced public transport system and the library parks, which themselves are public, community spaces. There is a consensus in Medellín that the previous lack of public spaces was evidence of the 'historical social debt'. These developments have nonetheless been controversial. Although participation by local communities was central to the PUIs, it is noteworthy that the projects which have resulted from these programmes are very similar to interventions that aimed to attract investment. It has also been argued that the creation of public spaces has been as much about extending the reach of the State as it has been about creating spaces for the community (Stienen, 2009; Roldán, 1999). High-profile buildings have required the installation of security and surveillance in areas where the State did not previously have a formalised grip on power (Stienen, 2009). Although this can be seen as progressive, many feel that given the State's use of militarised violence in these very areas at the same time that these plans were being developed, it does not yet have the legitimacy for such interventions to be unproblematic.

Observers have also questioned the extent to which the view of local people has been allowed to shape the outcomes of these projects, and what the parameters for participation were (Schwab, 2013; Sato, 2013). The informal map onto which these spaces were grafted persists, and the public spaces created in some cases cross the invisible borders demarcating the violent tensions between rival gangs, paramilitaries, and militia. Despite the construction of public spaces, Medellín remains one of the world's capitals of intra-urban displacement and the continuation of these tensions cannot be overlooked.

In comparable cities, the creation of public space has meant the destruction of informal, alternative, and subaltern ways of seeing the city. In Bogotá, for instance, the construction of public space 'allowed for the recovery of hundreds of kilometres of sidewalks previously occupied

DOI: 10.1057/9781137397362.0008

by street pedlars' (Castro and Echeverri, 2011: 98). In Medellín, a more 'hybrid' approach to informality that recognised the importance of informal markets and spaces to the city's identity, vibrancy, and economy was adopted, notably in the Hueco district in the centre of the city, where informal traders continue to dominate the pavement alongside the Parque Botero (Lopez and Kuc, 2009). Similarly, the upgrading of informal settlements, most notably in the Moravia and Juan Bobo districts, was the result of a long and carefully negotiated participatory process which resulted in high levels of resettlement (Sato, 2013).

For the policies in Medellín to be acceptable to and supported by the elites, they had to appeal to elite sensibilities. Art has been an important component of the policies to change the skin of the city and conspicuously invest in poorer areas. The architects I interviewed were passionate about this. 'This is what it should be like,' said one. 'Look at these buildings we've made – they're beautiful. And poorer people should have beautiful things too.'[4] The Parque Botero and the dramatically urbane and avant-garde architecture that has been brought to former no-go areas are the most visible changes in the city. However, cultural workers are sceptical: 'They're extending their power, and their right to define what art is,' said one theatre director.[5] He continued: 'Do you really think people from *las comunas* are going to go to the international tango festival?'

Although the grand infrastructural investments do reflect the classical tastes that would be associated with the elites, there are also a number of NGO and participatory cultural projects that perhaps belie this characterisation of Medellín's transformation. The prize-winning libraries that were designed by leading international architects also house exhibitions of art projects dedicated to the memory of the violence, such as a photo exhibition by teenagers that represents their emotional response to living with violence. The local television station Tele Medellín also showcases community artists, and its slogan '*Aquí te ves*' ['See yourself here'] clearly articulates its mission to reflect real life across the city.

The evidence on the use of these public spaces, and on whether these interventions have created new spaces for community contact, is so far inconclusive (Brand and Dávila, 2011; Schwab, 2013). The public spaces created – library parks, public parks, and sculpture parks – are inspired by the Barcelona model of urban regeneration, while at the same time speaking to the analysis of Medellín's woes, specifically the diagnosis of the violence as being rooted in the historical social debt. The questions that have been asked of other regeneration projects can

DOI: 10.1057/9781137397362.0008

be asked of Medellín's regeneration: Is this a reassertion of elite power and tastes, a project to extend the State, or a set of policies aimed more at attracting inward investment than promoting social and economic inclusion? However, there are issues specific to cities in the global South that have tended not to influence theoretical frameworks for understanding urban regeneration, which are apt to draw on examples from the North. Community participation, also a theme in urban studies in the North, takes on a different meaning in the context of the transition to democracy. Although economic development, however defined, is the goal of urban regeneration policies around the globe, in the global South the degree of poverty, inequality, and exclusion and the prominence of informality change the terms of this debate.

Participation and economic development

There are many ways in which the policies of social urbanism in Medellín replicate those of successful model cities around the world, most of them in the global North. The focus on infrastructure and branding in particular can be seen as strategies to put Medellín on the global investment map. However, there are important local specificities, in particular the violence but also development issues, that are challenges in cities across the global South (Robinson, 2006) and that distinguish social urbanism in this region from its European, Antipodean, and North American inspirations. High levels of inequality, informality, and poverty present a radically different socioeconomic context in which to roll out model urban regeneration. In addition, the political context in Latin America in the 1990s and the early twenty-first century was one of recovering from the 'lost decade' of the 1980s, consolidating democracy, and recognising the continent's plurality, in particular demands from indigenous movements spurred on by the 500th anniversary in 1992 of Columbus' conquest. The urban polices described above are, therefore, articulating with very different political concerns than those present in the global North.

As such, socioeconomic development 'from below' and inclusion of the informal economy are on the agenda in cities in the global South in a far more significant way than they are in post-industrial contexts. Economically, the need to address poverty and indigence is important not only in terms of rights but in terms of bolstering internal consumption, and economic development from below becomes a central concern of regeneration. Similarly, education policy, which in the rubric of urban

DOI: 10.1057/9781137397362.0008

regeneration policies in the North has been about persuading would-be investors of the skills of the local workforce, in the Latin American context faces the challenge of extending education provision to areas where there are no schools, with attendant debates around cultural and State dominance. In a city where more than 60 per cent of the economy is informal, exploring barriers to formal sources of credit, work, and business support is the focal point of development strategies.

The diversity of the population and a colonial history which continues to frame political power bring added complexities and urgency to questions of the participation and inclusion of marginalised citizens (Watson, 2009). In this context, participatory planning practices can amount to a 'clash of rationalities' (Watson, 2009: 2259), as the increasingly technological, marketised nature of institutions and systems of governance in city planning has created a breach between planners and 'the everyday lives of a marginalised and impoverished urban population surviving largely under conditions of informality' (Watson, 2009: 2260). In a post-Fordist context, decentralisation and participation have been strongly criticised as mechanisms to 'dump' (Brush, 2002) responsibilities previously taken on by the State on citizens, who under the rubric of 'participation' will labour, without pay, for very-little decision-making power. However, in the context of 'post-neoliberal', pluri-cultural Latin America, participation, and the legal and political frameworks to encourage it, have also been part of the resistance to the social costs that the continent bore during the 1980s (Maclean, 2013; 2014b). Participation can be a political strategy to extend public institutions to areas and people otherwise excluded from the ambit of formal politics, but in a context where these institutions tend to be seen as the domain of specific, often elite, interests (Simone, 2002), such involvement may not be progressive.

With the recognition that population growth across the world will not only mostly be in cities but in cities in the 'developing' world (Watson, 2009), the planning practices of cities in the global South have themselves become models, particularly with regard to participation, inclusion, and sustainability. The Brazilian cities of Porto Alegre and Curitiba have become reference points for participation and sustainable socio-economic development, and Rio de Janeiro's Favela–Bairro project has been seen as a model for dealing with informality. These cities are functioning in the globalised, neoliberal reality in which cities around the world are competing for investment, but these policies also reflect Latin American political challenges of diversity, inclusion, and integration of

DOI: 10.1057/9781137397362.0008

the informal economy. In 1990, a year after the election to power of the Workers Party, Porto Alegre adopted a Participatory Budget Scheme; a number of meetings were held throughout the year to ensure citizen accountability in the planning process and also citizen input into the participation process (De Sousa Santos, 1998; Novy and Leubolt, 2005). Similarly, Rio's Favela–Bairro programme takes a participatory approach to the upgrading of formal settlements and includes a focus on socio-economic development in order to reduce inequalities across the city (Riley et al., 2001). Although widely praised, Rio's programme has been argued to represent the limits of the meaningful participation that can be granted to citizens in a project with such clear aims (Riley et al., 2001).

Participation is at the core of Medellín's social urbanism and has been particularly evident in the participatory budget, inspired by the Porto Alegre model, and the PRIMED informal settlement upgrading scheme, inspired by Rio's Favela–Bairro programme. Participatory budgeting was first implemented by Mayor Juan Gómez Martínez in 1998. It was further developed by Fajardo into the Participatory Planning and Budgeting Programme, which aimed to bring government and planning in general closer to the citizenry and civil society, and to legitimate local government and promote transparency. A proportion of the budget for each neighbourhood is allocated for organisations to bid for project contracts, and the decision of which contracts are awarded funds is taken by a panel that includes community members. The amounts involved in this process almost doubled, from 59 million Colombian pesos in 2004 to more than 100 million in 2008 (Valencia et al., 2009).

More than an economic initiative, participatory budgeting is a political initiative designed to empower communities to determine their own priorities and increase the transparency of how funds are spent (Uran, 2010). The specific ways in which the participatory budget is implemented and the kinds of programme that it supports remain contentious. In particular, there is potential for these processes to be dominated by powerful, and violent, members of the community. Nevertheless, this initiative overturns decades of development in which investment was steered by elites who did not understand the priorities of people in the *comunas*.

Programmes funded by the participatory budget include art and theatre exhibitions dedicated to memory, community kitchens, and football parks. Whilst these do in a sense include and support participation – and change the political subject into one who makes proposals rather

DOI: 10.1057/9781137397362.0008

than just demands – at the same time they fundamentally change the dynamic between citizens and the State. Community leaders complained that participatory budgeting had turned them into fund raisers: whereas before they did community work, now they just fill out forms. One interviewee put it very clearly: 'If I get money from the local government, who is my boss? I'm not working for the communities anymore; I'm working for the State.'[6] The participatory budget neatly illustrates the tensions between promoting inclusion and cooptation by the State.

Various informal settlement improvement programmes carried out during the 1990s and the early twenty-first century have also been praised for being effective and adopting a participatory approach (Bredenoord and van Lindert, 2010). The projects in Medellín exhibit the tensions inherent in participatory approaches to development, which have to marry the technical requirements and objectives of the project with community ownership and participation. For instance, two of the main aims of the Programa de Mejoramiento Integral de Barrios [Integral Slum Improvement Programme – PMIB)] were '1) applying an efficient and flexible planning procedure based on technical criteria, 2) fostering community consensus and participation in generating secure living conditions' (Sato, 2013: 5–6). This tension was taken fully on board as the expert architects and technicians collaborated with sociologists and anthropologists during a dedicated period of fieldwork to get to know the neighbourhoods, which included daily visits to affected households. The head of the project, Carlos Montoya, claims that 'negotiation and rapport, not imposition was the most fundamental "tool" of the project' (Sato, 2013: 17).

There were, almost inevitably, problems with this approach that are predicted by the literature on participation and development. 'The community' is, of course, not a homogeneous whole, and disputes over the direction of a project are inevitable. In the context of high levels of violence and intra-urban displacement, a participatory approach risks exacerbating tensions and power relations already present. It was found that paramilitary groups used the projects to demand *vacunas* ['vaccines', the slang for protection money] as well as jobs and direct participation in the benefits (Betancur, 2007). Community leaders complain that despite attempts at participation, the needs of the area are not sufficiently taken into account, traditional public spaces are not respected, and there is not enough follow-up.

DOI: 10.1057/9781137397362.0008

Socioeconomic development from below

Reflecting both the need for a city to be competitive in the global economy and the post-neoliberal turn in Latin America, Medellín has become known as a city of competitiveness and solidarity (*'Medellín: Ciudad competitiva y solidaria'*) and the most educated city (*'la más educada'*) (Fajardo Valderrama, 2007). These slogans are visible on panels and posters throughout the city and were created by Mayor Fajardo and his administration. The aim is to create a more inclusive economy by encouraging cooperation and alliances between informal and formal businesses, and associations within communities that can bid for public contracts. Many of the policies employed to these ends are inspired by the northern Italian and Basque cooperative models (Bateman et al., 2011). In addition to support for community associations and micro-enterprises, there are larger-scale initiatives to encourage inclusive economic development. Various business incubators have been set up with funds from local government and business associations. The Medellín 'Cluster City' programme – an initiative of the local government and the Medellín Chamber of Commerce – consists of six strategic clusters: electric power; textiles/apparel, fashion design; construction; business tourism, fairs and conventions; medical and dental services; and technology, information and communication technologies. These foci have been chosen as a way to build an inclusive city whose development is for all its citizens, as well as to enable Medellín to attract investment (Medellín Ciudad Cluster, n.d.). There is also an extensive education and training programme targeted towards youth in the *comunas* who are deemed at risk of gang involvement.

The aim of building an inclusive economy has been part of the development and use of the new urban infrastructure. Among the programmes to promote economic inclusion are the CEDEZOs. These centres, located in the library parks, are information points that unite all the potential services available to support small and micro-entrepreneurs in the *comunas*. They provide information about potential sources of credit, training, and small business competitions that can result in contracts with the city's chain stores. The CEDEZOs address information gaps and the difficulties in accessing mainstream markets and have been successful in identifying entrepreneurs capable of making the crucial transition from a local, informal micro-enterprise to a small business that can reach the mainstream market (Bateman et al., 2011).

DOI: 10.1057/9781137397362.0008

As part of the drive to encourage small businesses to link more with the mainstream, communities have been supported in creating associations so that they can bid for contracts on public works. Examples of such associations cover catering, child care, and building work. Approaching public works in this way facilitates local job creation and changes the perception of cronyism in the allocation of public works contracts. In addition, there is a high-profile campaign, including local government support and a public service television campaign, to encourage the formation of cooperatives, as opposed to individual, informal micro-enterprises.

Medellín: *la más educada*

Education has taken centre stage in Medellín's social urbanism, both to address the exclusion seen to be a cause of the violence and to create a more inclusive, competitive economy. This has been intimately linked with urban developments. Under the Fajardo administration, 10 new colleges were built, and 40 per cent of the annual budget went to education. The description of these policies indicates the centrality of education to the social urbanism programme:

> We are investing 40 per cent of our budget on education and this year we built, among other things, 10 new schools for Medellín, really beautiful, well-equipped buildings located in the most neglected areas of our city, and equipped with all the necessary tools for children and young people to see the world in a different way, many of these schools have similar standards or better than any private school in the city. (Fajardo Valderrama, 2007)

Education is seen as central to the inclusion of people in the *comunas*, both to improve possibilities for upward mobility and to increase political awareness. The emphasis on education has extended to adult learning and NGO programmes, and there have been a number of funded scholarships that allow students from the *comunas*, particularly community leaders, to get places at prestigious private universities.

Underpinning the increased investment in education is an agreement among the city's leaders that education is the most important investment that can be made. The GEA has sponsored university places, as have the universities themselves. Various NGOs have undertaken projects that fall outside the remit of the State, such as adult education projects and community learning projects.

DOI: 10.1057/9781137397362.0008

The levels of continuing support for projects that invest in development and education vary. There is an acceptance of the need for continued training and support to address the barriers to accessing market opportunities in such an unequal city, but the resources available to do this, and the best way to achieve it, are in question. Projects such as those by the Sub-Secretariat for Women that take a political approach to addressing the barriers to women's participation in the market tend to take a long-term approach. This approach includes training in group formation and leadership and continued support as the project develops over the years. Private companies are encouraged to become involved in voluntary partnering schemes with smaller enterprises. Whilst these policies have created the political space for economic inclusion to be on the agenda, doubts are raised as to the long-term compatibility of a solidarity economy with competitiveness at the global scale. As one activist academic claimed, 'I worked for the Chamber of Commerce for years and I never heard a single person question the "bottom line" in terms of the profitability of their company.'[7]

Conclusion

Medellín's social urbanism is explicitly inspired by model cities around the world, and as such can be seen as one of the many urban rebranding exercises that cities across the globe, and in particular 'secondary cities', have undertaken to attract inward investment. The iconic buildings, mass transport systems, public spaces, and public art come from a consistent palette of policies that have been implemented in cities as diverse as Glasgow, Vancouver, and Abu Dhabi. However, in the context of Medellín, with its high levels of violence, inequality, and indigency, these policies take on a different meaning. They were implemented in the context of the city's commitment to addressing the historical social debt, which was the prominent discourse in understanding the city's violence, and the consequent need to change the skin of the city, which entailed a redesign of the city to allow a more inclusive society and economy. As a city in the global South, Medellín had to deal with issues associated with development, including informality, high rates of poverty, and inequality. Moreover, the political context in Latin America – a region moving on from the ravages of 1980s neoliberalism and continuing to consolidate democracy after the revolutions and coups of the twentieth

DOI: 10.1057/9781137397362.0008

century – meant that participation and decentralisation, again perhaps textbook features of urban regeneration, had a particular significance, and were supported by a different range of institutions.

The claim that the policies of social urbanism are responsible for the decline in the city's violence are not generally made by those who were directly involved in designing or implementing social urbanism or related policies. In terms of analyses of urban violence, high levels of inequality and exclusion can not only underpin violence but also be construed as violent in themselves, and interventions to address these factors are clearly relevant to a social approach to reducing urban violence. However, a more nuanced idea of the relationship between levels of urbanisation and violence takes into account power, and centring the analysis on power, it is not clear whether these interventions redressed power imbalances or were actually an exercise in reinforcing and legitimating State, and elite, power. It cannot be forgotten that in the middle of all the policies to address the city's inequality, the national government launched two military strikes on civilian populations in Medellín, in areas which went on to be the focus of progressive urban development policies.

It is impossible to draw a direct connection between the urban interventions in Medellín and the reduction in violence in the city. If it is accepted that violence is about power, then the questions to ask in terms of the relationship between social urbanism and violence is how social urbanism changed, or represented a change in, the way power was constructed – who was able to obtain power and how it was maintained. In designing and implementing each of the policies that define social urbanism, a balance was struck between a continuation of elite interests and more progressive elements. Looking in more detail at the processes behind these policies will provide the context needed to understand how the political urban landscape has changed. There is indeed a tension among the varying aims motivating social urbanism, and in particular between attracting investment and promoting inclusion and diversity, although these aims can coincide. The interplay of these tensions creates a multiplicity of political spaces that have to be understood in the context of the dynamics of change. If violence is understood politically, then the potential of social urbanism to address violence has also to be examined in political terms, which is the subject of the following two chapters.

DOI: 10.1057/9781137397362.0008

Notes

1   Said in an interview with Agence EFE, reported in Semana, 13 December 2010. Available at: http://www.semana.com/nacion/articulo/una-ciudad-avanzada-no-pobres-pueden-moverse-carro-sino-incluso-ricos-utilizan-transporte-publico/125258-3

2   Academic and activist, interview, 24 July 2012.

3   Drawing on Neil Smith's work on New York, the idea of urban revanchism is based on the Revanchists of nineteenth-century Paris, who were 'determined to reinstate the bourgeois order with a strategy that fused militarism and moralism with claims about restoring public order on the streets' (Slater 2010: 667).

4   Architect and business leader, interview, 30 July 2012.

5   Cultural worker and activist, interview, 30 July 2012.

6   Community activist, interview, 25 July 2012.

7   Academic, interview, 2 August 2012.

DOI: 10.1057/9781137397362.0008

4

Behind the Miracle

Abstract: *This chapter analyses the political and economic changes, discourses, and dynamics that allowed leftist community leaders, social organisations, and activists to sit at a table with the city's elites to develop and eventually implement social urbanism. During the 1990s, a number of changes at the global and national scales influenced narco-traffic and the struggles between guerrilla, paramilitary, and State actors in Colombia, and the Medellín Miracle needs to be understood in the context of the complex history of Colombia's trajectory towards democracy. Key points in this trajectory include electoral reform and, crucially, the country's new Constitution in 1991, but these steps have been accompanied by many other influences that have either reinforced or attenuated Colombia's democratic progress both politically and economically, and the political processes behind the miracle in Medellín reflect these dynamics of progress and revanchism.*

Keywords: business and industry; Colombian Constitution; democratisation; paramilitarism; Plan Colombia; political space

Maclean, Kate. *Social Urbanism and the Politics of Violence: The Medellín Miracle*. Basingstoke: Palgrave Macmillan, 2015. DOI: 10.1057/9781137397362.0009.

DOI: 10.1057/9781137397362.0009

The previous chapter detailed the specifics of social urbanism in Medellín in the context of international models of urban regeneration. The results of these policies have garnered international attention, in particular on the transport systems, public spaces, and innovative architecture. Compromiso Ciudadano, the political party headed by Sergio Fajardo that was to break the Conservative/Liberal hegemony by winning the mayoral elections in 2003 and go on to implement the social urbanism agenda, started as a social movement. It developed in the context of President Gaviria's 1991 Consejería Presidencial para Medellín [Presidential Programme for Medellín], which focused attention on the city's problems and dedicated resources to exploring potential solutions. In the same year, Colombia's new Constitution was ratified, which changed the political landscape and the way that participation and political dialogue were conceived of in the formal institutional context. Crucially, in terms of the implementation of the social urbanism agenda, diagnoses of the economic crisis by the Monitor Group[1] and the need to attract foreign investment to Medellín resonated with progressive agendas to address the root causes of the violence.

Underlying the present analysis of the Medellín Miracle is an exploration of how these policies relate to changes in the way that violence and power are associated in the city. This chapter and the next reflect on the processes behind the rise to power of Compromiso Ciudadano and social urbanism. These processes include the development of new political spaces, discourses, and articulations of various interests that have emerged over this period and changed the way that power is acquired, exercised, and maintained in Medellín. The fora that opened up represented a reconfiguration of the political landscape, which allowed interests that had formerly been viciously competing to come together. These processes themselves could be argued to have in part addressed the city's historical social debt and changed the political skin of the city. However, within these discourses can be found both progressive and revanchist interpretations and diagnoses of the violence of Medellín. That multiple interests could unite around the policies that made the miracle is at once the success of this process and the threat to its continuation.

This chapter introduces the changes at the global and national scales which have influenced narco-traffic and the struggles between guerrilla, paramilitary, and State actors in Colombia. It then places the Medellín Miracle in the complex history of Colombia's trajectory towards democracy and negotiations with armed groups in the ongoing conflict. The

DOI: 10.1057/9781137397362.0009

reform of the electoral system in 1988 so that mayors were elected by popular vote rather than appointed by governors and, crucially, the country's new Constitution in 1991 represent clear steps on the path towards democracy that Colombia has been on since the end of the Frente Nacional. This trajectory has been accompanied by multiple other influences that have either reinforced or attenuated democratic progress both politically and economically. Economic recession and neoliberal reforms, globalisation, NGOisation, and the US war on drugs have all influenced political dynamics in Colombia, as power in the country reconfigures and the established elites react (Carroll, 2011). The political processes behind the miracle in Medellín reflect these dynamics of progress and revanchism. This chapter analyses the political-economic changes and discourses that allowed leftist community leaders, social organisations, and activists to sit at a table with the city's protectionist economic elites and explore the contours and fault lines of the evolving political landscape.

Democratisation and violence in Colombia

Over the period from the recognition of the crisis of violence to the election of Compromiso Ciudadano and the implementation of social urbanism, a number of changes in the global and national political context affected the development of Colombia's long-running civil conflict and the role of narco-traffic within it. In the late 1990s, a plan was developed by President Pastrana to end the country's armed conflict and deal with narco-related violence. Whilst military support and counter-insurgency were part of this plan, the focus, inspired by the Marshall Plan, was socioeconomic development (Inkster and Comolli, 2012). However, this plan, after negotiations with the United States, became known as 'Plan Colombia' and was more focused on US aid and assistance against narco-traffic and insurgency, military intervention, support against specifically left-wing insurgent groups, and coca eradication than Pastrana originally intended (Petras, 2000; Stokes, 2001). Since the turn of the century, the United States has supported the Colombian government with a budget of more than US$600 million a year, which has mostly been in military aid (Isaacson, 2014). After 9/11, the declaration of the 'War on Terror' meant that Colombia's strife became a lower priority for the United States than the perceived threats from Iraq and Afghanistan

DOI: 10.1057/9781137397362.0009

(Vaicius and Isacson, 2003). Nevertheless, US assistance to Colombia increased. The additional funds and political support strengthened the Colombian government militarily and legitimised its stance against the FARC, ELN, and left-wing insurgents. The association of narco-violence with the Marxist guerrilla groups that underpins US military support in Colombia has been assessed as inaccurate by its own agencies (Stokes, 2001). The assumption that the guerrillas are the main perpetrators has also been strongly criticised for failing to deal adequately with paramilitary violence, which, since 1990, has accounted for the highest number of conflict and narco-related deaths in Colombia (Isaacson, 2014).

Plan Colombia supported Uribe's anti-FARC stance and 'iron fist' approach to Colombia's conflict. Nevertheless, peace negotiations with the FARC took place throughout this period. The first peace agreement was signed with the FARC in 1984, after negotiations led by President Betancur, and there have been multiple attempts at peace negotiations at the national level since then. Pastrana's peace negotiations, which ultimately failed, involved ensuring a demilitarised zone, a greater focus on socioeconomic development, and a stronger stance against paramilitary groups. These negotiations were strongly criticised by all sides and failed when violence resumed (Castañeda, 2003). President Santos, elected in 2010, has re-opened negotiations with the FARC, which is seen as a clear change in direction from the policies of his predecessor, Uribe. Whilst popular support for peace negotiations with the FARC is strong, so is support for Uribe's approach, as was evidenced in the Colombian elections of 2014, in which Uribe's party, Centro Democractico, made significant gains (BBC, 2014).

Extradition treaties with the United States have been crucial to political dynamics in Colombia, given the immense political and economic power of those involved in narco-traffic and the associated armed groups. After high-profile extraditions during the 1980s, the existing extradition treaty was declared unconstitutional in 1987 by the Colombian Supreme Court. This decision was allegedly influenced by the group Los Extraditables, whose members included Pablo Escobar. Its aim was to object to any extradition treaty with the Unites States, under the slogan 'We prefer a tomb in Colombia to prison in the US'. The 1991 Constitution initially banned extradition to the United States, but this was reversed in 1997.

The oscillations over extradition to the United States indicate that it was a political as much as a judicial matter. Lack of extradition to the United States in a sense appeased Los Extraditables, but as the United

DOI: 10.1057/9781137397362.0009

States became more important to Colombian development, with Plan Colombia, free-trade agreements, and the additional support that came from Uribe's relationship with President George W. Bush and the 'War on Terror', the number of extraditions to the United States increased. Although it has been alleged that Uribe's government was more 'flexible' in its extradition of paramilitary actors (*New York Times*, 2004), the number of key players extradited has changed the Colombian political territory, has reduced the power of armed actors, and indicates the growing independence of the judiciary (Browitt, 2001).

Over this period, two legal frameworks have been evoked to enable the demobilisation of armed groups: Law 418 of 1997 and the Justice and Peace Law of 2005. Law 418 grants an amnesty to those willing to demobilise, and this amnesty was extended by Uribe to allow the government to engage with groups lacking political status, such as the paramilitary group Autodefensas Unidas de Colombia [United Self-Defence Forces of Colombia – AUC] (Hylton, 2006: 105). It has been alleged that this process has allowed people suspected of serious human rights violations to be granted amnesty, which violates international law (Hylton, 2006; CJA, n.d.). The Justice and Peace Law of 2005 regulates the granting of amnesty and attempts to offer incentives for peace whilst also respecting the need for justice, reparation, and memory (CJA, n.d.). However, it failed, as Amnesty International alleged, 'to comply with international standards on victims' right to truth, justice and reparation' (Amnesty International, 2005).

Bolstered by America's Plan Colombia, Colombian military force has been used to attack the FARC and associated groups in rural and urban areas (Diaz, 2007). In a further example of the blurred line between paramilitary and military forces (Filippone, 1994; Ceballos Melguizo and Cronshaw, 2001; BBC, 2013), paramilitary groups, which have always been used to defend property interests against leftist insurgents, also played a part in this process and in Operación Orión and Operación Mariscal. It has also been argued that the steep decline in Medellín's homicide rate was the result of a 'paramilitary peace' (Hylton, 2008) and that 'simply put, homicides in Medellín dropped during the period of Fajardo's administration because Don Berna [paramilitary leader] and paramilitary forces, facilitated by the State, controlled the city' (Tubb, 2013: 637). The motives of the paramilitaries are said to coincide with the aims to brand the city on the global stage. An Amnesty International report on the decommissioning of paramilitary actors in the mid-1990s

DOI: 10.1057/9781137397362.0009

indicated that Bloque Cacique Nutibara [Cacique Nutibara Block – BCN], one of the city's most prominent paramilitary groups,

> stated that they had partly been responsible for a fall in homicides in Medellín and that this ensured 'the necessary climate so that investment, particularly foreign, which is fundamental if we do not want to be left behind by the engine of globalization, returns, is encouraged, and productive, and long-term employment can be generated'. (Amnesty International, 2005: 31–32)

The reduction of violence in Medellín is intricately entwined with these multiple processes of constitutional change, developing relationships with the United States, and the growth of paramilitary power, which underscores the difficulty and complexity in attributing the city's transformation to social urbanism. The changes in Medellín also reflect the processes at the national level, which have fluctuated between a heavy-handed approach towards establishing State control via the use of military force and the focus on socioeconomic development as a way to achieve peace. People directly involved in the development and implementation of social urbanism are far more circumspect in their claims about the effects of its policies than the international press, and stress that 'Our problems are very profound, and it's not like they get solved in eight years, and one city alone can't solve them either. Medellín is not isolated from the national and regional context, which continues to be very complicated.'[2] Not only is it necessary to view Medellín's transformation in the national context to better understand the political processes that went on there, but the processes in Medellín also shed light on these evolving political dynamics.

The dynamics of democratisation and the reassertion of elite and State control can also be seen in economic developments since the peak of violence in Medellín in the early 1990s. This was a time of economic crisis in Colombia, and Medellín, home to some of the country's main industries, felt the effects of de-industrialisation and recession more than most cities. Economic pressures and changes – specifically recession, neoliberalisation, and, crucially, the need to attract foreign direct investment – have driven political change in Colombia since the 1990s and are intimately involved in developments in Medellín. The 1991 Constitution, in addition to facilitating greater political openness and inclusion, established powers to enact the recommendations of the Washington Consensus and included provisions to facilitate the attraction of foreign direct investment by reducing import tariffs, scaling

DOI: 10.1057/9781137397362.0009

back the public sector, privatising national industries, and opening 'free commerce' zones (Browitt, 2001). Whilst these policies, until the recession of the late 1990s, maintained the historical strengths of Colombian national economic indicators (Gilbert, 1997; Arbeláez et al., 2001; Villar and Rincón, 2000), their effects also reflect the consequences of such policies elsewhere: growing inequality, informalisation, and exclusion of the poorest (Isaza Castro, 2003; Spagnolo and Munevar, 2008). Global economic forces, and in particular the need (per the Washington Consensus) to attract foreign investment, are at once an opportunity and a threat to economic elites. This was certainly the case in Medellín, where business elites are renowned for their insularity. The way that they negotiated global developments is key to understanding the politics behind the Medellín Model, and the dynamics of democratisation, reassertion of State power, and violence that accompanied it.

Progress and revanchism in Medellín

Models of urban regeneration, including some of those discussed in the previous chapter, have been criticised for facilitating an elite revanchism, despite being ostensibly predicated on the idea of the 'right to the city' (MacLeod, 2002; Smith, 2002, 2012; Slater, 2004). From the military operations of Uribe to the insistence on good behaviour on public transport exemplified in the 'Cultura Metro' campaign, the re-establishment of elite power can be seen throughout the Medellín Miracle. That fact should not detract from the achievements of the progressive movements at work in Medellín over this time, which will be explored in the next chapter, but rather emphasises how the reinforcement of elite control was part of the political space that had to be negotiated. In recent years, there have been fears in the city that the balance that had to be struck with the powers-that-be to effect change may be being jeopardised.

The Medellín Miracle is in some ways based on progressive ideas of reducing inequality and promoting inclusion. In other senses, though, the politics that made social urbanism possible includes a desire by elites to take back their city and, in their terms, re-take the responsibility for stewardship that historically has defined them. This is apparent in the discourses, spaces, and articulations of various interests that are involved in the city's transformation, which were enabled by the broader political-economic context in Colombia.

DOI: 10.1057/9781137397362.0009

The 1991 Constitution was, according to many involved in Compromiso Ciudadano, the 'without which not' of the Medellín Miracle. As one civil servant in the Medellín mayor's office put it in 2012:

> The Constitution of ninety-one marks a break in two things: participation and the concept of power. Before this, participation in Colombia was seen as subversive – it was more attached to being on the left, being a guerrilla, or part of organisations that were against the State. But then, in ninety-one, in the Constitution participation appears as a right.[3]

The Constitution offered a framework, ratified at the highest level, that in part enabled community leaders, NGOs, and social movements to have a seat at the table with members of the traditional political and business elite in Medellín. The Constitution redistributed power between the executive and the judiciary, guaranteed social rights to minority groups, and encouraged participatory democracy and social inclusion (Palacios, 2006). Specifically, it broadened the definition of rights recognised in Colombia to include socioeconomic rights and community rights, and explicitly clarified the role of NGOs and the duty of the State to recognise their political legitimacy (Flórez, 1997). These rights have been further reinforced insofar as the Constitutional Court established in 1991, unlike its predecessor, has taken into account demands for rights and inclusion from marginalised groups, as the Constitution guarantees human rights, and writs of protection can be ordered if these are being violated (García-Herreros, 2012; Bejarano and Pizarro Leongómez, 2002).

The Constitution was also a further step in unshackling formal politics from the Liberal/Conservative hegemony, which Compromiso Ciudadano was the first party in Medellín to break with. The elected members of the Constituent Assembly represented a much broader spectrum of political interests, and this can be considered a success in itself given the momentum to loosen the two main parties' grip on power since the Frente Nacional[4] (García-Herreros, 2012). Nevertheless, and despite these progressive steps, the Constitution of 1991 has been described as one of many attempts by the 'oligarchy to forge a stable modern nation-State without undermining their dominant position in the Colombian polity' (Browitt, 2001: 1063). This pattern of democratisation – in civic and political terms – accompanied by neoliberal economic policy underpins the way that political and economic power changed in Medellín over this time. The greater recognition of social movements, community groups, and NGOs, many of which espoused 'radical'

DOI: 10.1057/9781137397362.0009

left-wing views that had been formerly excluded from Colombian politics, was accompanied by free-market economic reforms, which are associated with an increase in inequality and have been found in numerous cases to undermine social rights and democracy (e.g. Kurtz, 2004; Smith et al., 1994; Weyland, 2004). Nevertheless, the early 1990s marked an important confluence of the formulae given by international analysts to business elites to attract foreign investment and the desire on the part of progressive organisations to create a 'solidarity economy' and address the exclusions of Medellín's economic development.

The other vital piece of democratising legislation that strongly influenced the processes in Medellín over the 1990s was the institutionalisation of the popular election of mayors. In 1988, mayors were elected for the first time by popular vote rather than being appointed, as previously, by department governors (Dávila, 2009). This procedural change, combined with the decentralisation of economic and fiscal responsibilities stemming from the 1991 Constitution, meant that mayors had more autonomy and power, including the ability to raise taxes and execute institutional and budgetary reforms. This reform in leadership continued the trajectory the country had been on since the end of the Frente Nacional, from political elites who were removed from citizens to popular representation and participation. This development was also crucial in changing the political culture, and particularly important to Fajardo's election and leadership, as well as the development of Compromiso Ciudadano.

The Medellín Miracle and the development of the policies that came to be defined as social urbanism can be seen as part of Colombia's process of democratisation, a trajectory that has been violent and revanchist but has also opened up political spaces and processes that have challenged the way violence is implicated in the country's politics. In part, the changes in Medellín over the past 20 years can be seen as a distillation of these national processes. However, as the city that was by far the most beset by violence and, not unrelatedly, particularly hit by the economic crisis, Medellín had a prominent place in these processes, and was defined by President Gaviria in 1990 as the most important concern for the country as a whole. Particularly important in the context of Colombia, where regions differ so greatly and have always had a strong identity of their own, local elites, dynamics, and institutions shaped the pathway of these democratic processes.

DOI: 10.1057/9781137397362.0009

Changes in Medellín

The local processes in question were initiated primarily as a result of the recognition at the international, national, and local levels that Medellín's violence had reached a crisis point. This led to specific investments, programmes, and fora that, particularly in the context of the new Constitution and electoral reforms, changed political processes in the city. Crucially, another crisis was also in motion – the economic crisis – which was not unrelated to the violence but nevertheless had dimensions of its own. The reaction of business elites to the economic crisis – the way they understood it, the disputes they had around it, and the approaches, particularly on the need for foreign direct investment, that emerged – was crucial to the politics of the city and the way that coalitions between communities, radical political organisations, and business elites were possible.

The peak in violence in Medellín in the early 1990s was the crisis point which galvanised the city into action. The numbers were staggering, and people in Medellín can flesh out these figures with their memories of fear and defiance in the most violent city on Earth. This moment had a clear effect on the politics of the city, and the willingness of the elites to negotiate with those they had previously excluded was in part due to the crisis of violence: 'For a brief period (between 1993 and 1995) violence rose to such unprecedented levels that Medellín's economic elite and the city authorities (with the support of the national government) agreed to negotiate with lower class dwellers on the latters' terms' (Roldán, 2002: 144). One activist and academic involved in Compromiso Ciudadano confirms:

> Bombs, deaths, the most violent city in the world, a left-wing that cannot take power because it has no strength and a right-wing that's not governing, there is no alternative of a different government. So I think that all this created an enabling environment [for dialogue].[5]

Attacks in the exclusive area of El Poblado, where 'even young people from the upper classes died',[6] motivated the city's privileged classes to engage in city-wide dialogue about the crisis in violence . However, the time it took for the city's elites to be directly affected by and react to the violence testifies to the highly unequal geographical distribution of poverty and violence in the city.

DOI: 10.1057/9781137397362.0009

Two specific interventions enabled dialogue across this highly divided city. The Consejería Presidencial para Medellín was set up by President Gaviria in 1990 and involved resources and personnel from outside the city dedicated to resolving the crisis of violence. This programme marked the recognition of the crisis and also facilitated the political fora – in particular the Seminarios Alternativas para el Futuro de Medellín [Seminars on Alternatives for the Future of Medellín] – that were to result in the emergence of a new political party and the development of social urbanism. At the same time, a report by the influential Monitor Group on the status of the economy in Colombia and Medellín recommended opening up the economy and modernising its traditionally very closed structure (Monitor, 1994). This report, and the broader economic pressures that it represented, enabled the consensus with the traditional elites that enabled social urbanism to be implemented, but at the same time encouraged the revanchism implicit in the policies of social urbanism that many fear is gaining the upper hand.

Consejería Presidencial para Medellín

In 1990, the Colombian president elect, Cesar Gaviria, identified the violence and cartel activity in Medellín as the country's biggest challenge. As Gaviria announced at a news conference shortly after returning from the United States: 'The country's gravest problem now is violence in Medellín, and this will require special treatment from my government, a treatment that transcends just military, police and public order measures' (APN, 1990). A report written in 1991 – *Medellín: Reencuentro con el Futuro* [Medellín: Re-encounter with the Future][7] – diagnosed the root causes of the violence as being related to inequality and poverty. This insight set a new agenda in terms of how the causes of violence were conceptualised in political debate on the subject. The Consejería Presidencial para Medellín was set up, with a special national government advisor, Maria Emma Mejía, in charge of developing solutions for the city. Mejía had a substantial budget from the Bogotá government and Antioquian business associations to support an ambitious social plan, including investment in housing and cultural programmes (*Semana*, 1990). This opened up new avenues of financial support for NGOs, social movements, and community groups, changing the political landscape in Medellín at a moment when the city's elites were under direct national pressure to find alternatives.

DOI: 10.1057/9781137397362.0009

The 1991 report, *Medellín: Reencuentro con el Futuro*, hence marked the recognition among Colombia's formal political leaders of the need to seriously address Medellín's problems. It was written by academics from Medellín's public universities – the University of Antioquia and the National University – various NGOs, and the UNDP (Rivera, 2006), and points out the structural underpinnings of the violence, which came to be known as the historical social debt owed to the excluded of the city, and its findings have defined the agenda since. Poverty and inequality, joblessness (particularly among the young), low levels of education, high levels of informal housing, and a lack of public spaces were all emphasised as causes of the high levels of violence (Rivera, 2006). In addition to setting a liberal agenda that drew causal associations between poverty, inequality, exclusion, and violence, the report itself, and the political spaces it opened up, marked a change in processes of power in the city.

The funding that had been made available, and the newly defined priorities in the 1991 report, created the political spaces in which coalitions could be formed. The discourse of the historical social debt permeated many of these initiatives, including the Foros Comunales [Community Fora] and Seminarios Alternativas para el Futuro de Medellín that took place between 1991 and 1995 and included political, community, and business leaders, as well as international organisations such as the UNDP and KFW Development Bank (Echeverría Ramírez and Bravo Giraldo, 2009). The participation of international policymakers, development organisations, and policy specialists allowed coalitions to be built and, crucially, financial support to be solicited from international organisations (*El Tiempo*, 1991).

The recognition that the city's violence had reached a crisis point also enabled these changes in the city's political fabric. After the first seminar, in 1991, the national newspaper *El Tiempo* described the event as drawing together

> the proposals and points of view of citizens, the State, industry, media, universities, and the military.... Although violence in the city persists, as does the scepticism, there is a commitment between many social, political, and economic groups to drive this process of the reconstitution of the city forward, as a piece of work of citizens' leadership. (*El Tiempo*, 1992)

This quotation indicates the commitment of various groups at the time and the broad base of participation that the seminars created. Various reports and policy working groups came out of the events of 1991,

DOI: 10.1057/9781137397362.0009

including working groups on key themes such as youth, employment, nutrition, and women's equality. These working groups generated innovative policies based on international experiences of building a more inclusive, participatory economy. Some of the policy programmes that resulted from these fora went on to be central facets of social urbanism. The Working Group on Space and Territory first discussed the Metrocable as a tourist initiative that could also be focused on connectivity within the city. Similarly, the Working Group for Employment discussed the importance of forming associations to improve livelihoods in the informal economy, and how these could articulate with debates on the mainstream economy. A number of policy programmes, including the PUIs discussed in Chapter 3 and the Programa de Núcleos de Vida Ciudadana [Cores of City Life Programme], also developed from these processes (Alcaldía de Medellín, 1996).

The policies, reports, and expertise that came out of these experiences were vital in creating the miracle of Medellín. They resulted in a crucial document, the Plan Estratégico para Medellín [Strategic Plan for Medellín] 1995–1998, that lists many of the policy innovations that were to become known as social urbanism. The plan defined 5 strategic lines and 106 projects, 40 of which were deemed to be high priority. Many of the remarkably wide range of organisations that participated in the seminars and discussions went on to have a role in various working groups and workshops dedicated to formulating projects and policies that would render these strategies viable (Echeverría Ramírez and Bravo Giraldo, 2009). Similarly, the Programa de Núcleos de Vida Ciudadana represents a radical break with the way the city had been envisaged before (Dapena Rivera, 2006). Its remit was to directly address the spatial distribution of poverty and underdevelopment in the city, which has been the most prominent feature of policies associated with Medellín's Miracle, and a theme that has been constant throughout the two decades since the crisis.

The Consejería Presidencial introduced an agenda that framed the Medellín Miracle, underpinned by the association between the city's violence and the city's social and economic problems. It also, in itself, was part of the radical changes in political processes, in the way that power was gained and maintained, in the city, which was arguably as influential in terms of the reduction in violence as the specific interventions of social urbanism. The processes by which political coalitions developed in these new spaces changed, and also represent change in, the political landscape.

DOI: 10.1057/9781137397362.0009

The economic crisis

The crisis of violence was not the only crisis facing Medellín in the early 1990s. The economic crisis, both from the global recession which had so affected Medellín and from the increasingly globalised nature of capital presented the opportunity for already successful elite families and businesses to increase their wealth. However, the economic crisis also threatened their position, by opening up historically protectionist networks, institutions, and mechanisms that had helped them establish and retain economic dominance. It divided the economic elites into a 'new' elite that wanted to engage with the opportunities brought by economic capital and the 'old' elite, who wanted to adopt more protectionist methods. There was a perception that attracting foreign direct investment to the city was essential if it was to compete globally, but also a recognition that this would be substantially impeded by the high levels of violence in the city, as well as the high-profile nature of this violence and the city's reputation for crime, narco-traffic, and corruption.

The influential Monitor Report *Competitive Advantages for Medellín*, was commissioned by Medellín's Chamber of Commerce as part of a broader report on Colombia as a whole which was published in 1994 (Monitor, 1994). The Medellín report was remarkably candid in its conclusion that the economic leaders of the city had to change to deal with the opportunities and threats that come with globalisation:

> Stagnant and reactionary mind-sets can never lead the firms that are demanded by the new world order. In fact, yesterday's men are not in a position to manage the complex realities of tomorrow. That is the great challenge that we are facing today: either we change or we disappear, obviously after our organizations have collapsed. (Camara de Comercio, n.d.: 28)

The conclusions of this report coincided with those of *Medellín: Re-encuentro con el Futuro*: that the city's inequality, limited development in certain areas, and exclusionary cultural attitudes were the problem. The report also concluded that making a world-class competitive city was everyone's business – 'government, business, workers, media and academics' (Camara de Comercio, n.d.: 29) – and emphasised that business leaders needed a new sense of responsibility and commitment to the city. The report explicitly advised forming coalitions with other political actors in the city to improve the economy and open more opportunities for business.

Specific recommendations to improve the global competitiveness of Medellín also aligned with the more social agenda proposed by the

DOI: 10.1057/9781137397362.0009

reports from the Consejería Presidencial, which focused on investment in mass education, clusters rather than specific industries, and building up Medellín's human resources. As the Chamber of Commerce of Medellín highlighted, the priorities were to:

> develop advanced human resources, overcome the deficiencies in infrastructure, better the internal conditions for the attraction of foreign direct investment. But perhaps the most important will be the development of a more assertive attitude towards learning and institutional modernisation. (Camara de Comercio, n.d.: 10)

These recommendations, essentially advocating modernisation, permitted a confluence between the agendas of progressive organisations, empowered by the new Constitution and the Consejería Presidencial, and those of traditional elites, who were galvanised into action by the pressure to address the violence. Crucially, business leaders were being made aware of the need for Medellín's economy to change structurally in the face of globalisation. However, business leaders and social movements had very different understandings of the problems in Medellín and motives for wanting change in the city, and the extent to which the collaboration of business elites in these political processes is about a genuine desire for change or about concern with the bottom line can be questioned.

The proposals of the Consejería Presidencial resonated with traditional elites' concerns that they are responsible for the stewardship of their region. The commitment to addressing exclusion in the city and redressing the historical social debt reinforces elite pride in the development of Antioquia, as much as it promotes the need for inclusion and social justice. Diagnoses of Colombia's and Medellín's violence made by prominent elite actors has attributed what is perceived as a breakdown in social order to elite influence being overshadowed, and the solution is that they need to take back the reins (see Restrepo Santamaria, 2011; Valenzuela Delgado, 1999). The fact that there was a convergence between the central discourses of social urbanism and this ethos of public service and stewardship among Medellín's elites was politically and financially necessary for the enactment of the policies of social urbanism. However, there are also concerns that the 'miraculous' transformation of Medellín, whilst for a while chiming with a progressive agenda, has in fact been driven by a revanchist elite who are consolidating their position.

Powerful business conglomerates and public companies provided the funding and support for the development of social urbanism. The organisation that is frequently referred to as having made the biggest difference in Medellín is Empresas Publicas de Medellín [Public Companies of Medellín – EPM]. EPM is one of the biggest and most powerful companies in Latin America. As a publicly owned company it is mandated to give 30 per cent of its annual net profit to the city's administration (Bateman et al 2011: 2), but as well as this financial contribution, the institution is the pride of Antioquia and is hugely politically significant. The resources made available to the municipality by EPM allowed the city to make the investments in infrastructure, including the Metrocable, libraries, and parks, and investment in education that came to define the miracle, and were, according to all the members of the Fajardo administration interviewed, an essential condition of social urbanism (Bateman et al., 2011).

However, the distinction between public ownership and elite control in Antioquia is not clear-cut. In 1995, under the mayoralty of Sergio Naranjo, the possibility of privatising EPM was raised in a report from the Ministry of Planning. This possibility was discussed over the following two years, but in addition to resistance from the workers' union, it provoked a massive mobilisation by the political class in Medellín. As one focus group participant commented: 'You should have seen El Poblado swing into action when that happened – they took to the streets!'[8] As did a number of members of the Council of Medellín itself (Varela Barrios, 2011).The vociferous calls for EPM to be retained as a public company are, however, as much to do with the close connection it has with the political class as with the provision of public utilities. Directorship of EPM is one of the portfolio of roles that define elite control of the city. Mayors of Medellín, and governors of Antioquia, have frequently also been involved in the stewardship of EPM, most notably Alvaro Uribe, who has been mayor, governor, and a director of EPM, as well as, of course, president of Colombia.

Nevertheless, the fact that EPM is public whilst enjoying a reputation as a well-managed company belies many neoliberal tenets about the role of the public sector in development. EPM has been key in extending infrastructure such as water, electricity, and telecommunications to marginalised areas of Medellín, including informal settlements and the rural areas within the formal jurisdiction of the city. However, the price of these services has frequently been challenged by community leaders, and EPM has been seen by some as an extension of the State – again, in a context where the State is one actor in a civil conflict and lacks legitimacy. As one cultural worker, slightly tongue in cheek, summarised, 'It's their slogan, "We're there" [*Estamos ahí*]. It's kind of threatening.'[9]

DOI: 10.1057/9781137397362.0009

As discussed in Chapter 2, there has been a history in Antioquia of businesses forming regionally defined associations to protect themselves from external threats and demonstrate their commitment to their region, for example the GEA and Pro-Antioquia. Both organisations have financed education programmes, business incubators, and other interventions associated with the Medellín Miracle. But this tradition of philanthropic investment and stewardship of their region is underpinned, in the words of Carlos Enrique Piedrahita, head of the Nutresa Group, by 'a philosophy of austere business ethics' (*Financial Times*, 2010). Despite business leaders finding common cause with social movements when dealing with the crises of violence and recession, this austere approach to business may eventually corrode the social aim of addressing exclusion and inequality that is central to the Medellín Miracle.

In the 1990s, business elites' traditional sense of stewardship of their region was also a reaction to the growing global concern at the time that corporations should demonstrate 'social responsibility'. This approach is exemplified in Pro-Antioquia's mission statement: 'to help in the construction of a more economically competitive and socially equitable region, in order to have an integrated and peaceful society with opportunities for everyone' (Pro-Antioquia, n.d.). The presence of strong business associations dedicated to the region has been one of the necessary conditions of the Medellín Miracle. The investment of money, time, and expertise from the business sector is a key characteristic of the city's 'solidarity economy'. But in the foundation of these organisations, we can also see that business interests – which have always aimed to protect elite control over assets as well as invest in the region – are being shored up by the general momentum of the economy. For example, although Pro-Antioquia was involved in Compromiso Ciudadano, a study by the Instituto Popular de Capacitación [Popular Capacitation Institute – IPC] of the business incubators that they sponsored concluded that they were using them primarily to continue to dominate private enterprise in the region. As the report states:

> The increased participation in the social sphere by the business sector is in stark contrast to the central momentum of labour policies which are based on reducing labour costs via flexibility and vertical integration of small and medium-sized production units. (Betancur et al., 2001: 249; my translation)

Whilst the interests of business when faced with the threats and opportunities posed by globalisation coincided with the priorities that had been

DOI: 10.1057/9781137397362.0009

generated by the Consejería Presidencial, the agenda that developed also allowed the recreation and reinforcing of power structures underpinning economic exclusion. There was also a sense among business leaders involved in the changing processes in Medellín that this was an opportunity to return to old values. In a focus group with business leaders in the city, this was made clear: 'This is what we're like,' said the head of a firm of architects. 'For years we have been associated with drugs and mafiosos, but the elites in this city have always invested in the poor. This is a place where someone's word was trusted, and where you looked after your workers – provided them with housing and good schools – we've always been like this.'[10]

The involvement of business organisations in Medellín's transformation was based on various overlapping motives: a commitment to the region's development that could be understood as a reaction to the crisis, a recognition that the economic structures of the city needed to change, and a reassertion of elite and paternalist values. In response to the economic developments, however, a divide emerged in the city's economic elites. The Monitor Group report stated that business leaders would have to open up to global forces, and subsequent developments in response to this report, including the establishment of the Economic Council for Medellín in 1995, supported its conclusions that the economy had to change fundamentally. In 1997, however, there was a rupture within the Economic Council between the traditional elite, who wanted to remain in Antioquia and keep power, and a newer type of entrepreneur who wanted to open up to globalisation. Despite this split, there was enough that resonated in the recommendations set out in the report about the need to open up and structurally change the economy and to invest in education to make the agenda developed in civil society politically feasible.

Conclusion

Exploring the processes behind social urbanism reveals what many involved in its development and implementation are happy to confirm: this was no overnight 'miracle'. Colombia's new Constitution, which reflected as well as instigated changes in the political landscape, and the economic pressures from globalisation opened up political spaces that enabled a resonance of ideas and the articulation of viewpoints that were

DOI: 10.1057/9781137397362.0009

hitherto excluded from mainstream debate. Medellín was particularly affected by the recession as well as the spectacular rates of violence that had developed. The Consejería Presidencial, along with the political and economic developments affecting the country as a whole, directly opened up the political spaces – the fora, seminars, and reports – that were to result in the success of the new political party Compromiso Ciudadano and social urbanism.

Given these developments, the political and economic power dynamics that had underpinned the rise to power of Medellín's violent actors – the cartel, paramilitaries, left-wing militia, and, in various guises, the State – began to change. Crucially, the notion of participation began to develop and become more prominent, and progressive organisations, including certain NGOs and community groups that had previously been considered to be against the State were brought into the fold of formal State institutions. Economic exclusion and underdevelopment came onto the agendas not only of these organisations but also of the city's business leaders, as they recognised the need to attract foreign direct investment. Whilst progressive forces could begin to take advantage of the spaces that opened up, the seeds of a revanchist opposition from the city's notoriously protectionist elites are also present in the discussions and reports that set the social urbanism agenda. Nevertheless, the elites' aim to reassert their stewardship of the city did coincide with the more liberal diagnoses of the groups that put together the reports, and this fact is crucial in understanding how Compromiso Ciudadano was able to implement its policies.

It is not possible to isolate interventions, factors, or people that directly affected the decline in violence. It is, however, possible to say that in this changing political context, we can see the beginnings of political relations and subjects changing in a way that potentially began to reform some of the political underpinnings of violence in Medellín. In the final chapter, I look at the use that was made of this developing political context by the newly empowered political actors that emerged.

Notes

1   The Monitor Group, founded in 1983 by a group of prominent economists at Harvard Business School, and since 2013 known as Monitor Deloitte,

DOI: 10.1057/9781137397362.0009

offers consultancy to organisations and governments on business strategy, economic development, and security.

2 Member of the Fajardo administration, interview, 8 August 2012.

3 Focus group, Sub-Secretariat for Participation, 17 July 2012.

4 Whilst the Liberal Party held 34 per cent of these seats, the Conservative Party polled only 7 per cent, and 'new' parties gained ground – notably the left-wing M19 Party (27 per cent) and the right-wing MSN (16 per cent) (García-Herreros, 2012: 239).

5 Academic and NGO activist, interview, 7 August 2012.

6 Academic and NGO activist, interview, 7 August 2012.

7 Dirección del Programa Presidencial para Medellín y su Área Metropolitana (1991), *Medellín: Reencuentro con el Futuro*, Bogotá: Presidencia de la República.

8 Focus group of business leaders, 25 July 2012.

9 Cultural worker, interview, 30 July 2012.

10 Focus group of business leaders, 25 July 2012.

DOI: 10.1057/9781137397362.0009

5
New Political Spaces

Abstract: *Despite the continued dominance in many ways of traditional elites, political spaces have emerged in Medellín over the last 20 years that have enabled different political actors to have a seat at the table, influence the agenda, and in some cases gain power within the formal mechanisms of local government. The contention here is that in these new political spaces is seen the real potential of the miracle, as they represent a disruption to the long-standing elite dominance of the city's politics and economy. This chapter explores the ways in which those who were involved in the seminars, working groups, and coalitions that emerged in the wake of the crisis were able to make use of these fora. A more participatory approach to politics developed over this time that challenged clientelism and the lack of a clear demarcation between formal and informal politics that had underpinned the prevalence of violence. The forms of leadership and power that emerged represent a change in the values that frame ideas of authority and power and in the role of violence in establishing authority.*

Keywords: community participation and development; Compromiso Ciudadano; gender; leadership; NGOs; radical education; women's movement

Maclean, Kate. *Social Urbanism and the Politics of Violence: The Medellín Miracle.* Basingstoke: Palgrave Macmillan, 2015. DOI: 10.1057/9781137397362.0010.

Despite the continued dominance in many ways of traditional elites, political spaces have emerged in Medellín over the last 20 years that have changed the city's political landscape. This chapter focuses on the organisations that were involved in the fora and processes that opened up in Medellín during the 1990s, and, in particular, on the formation of the political party Compromiso Ciudadano, whose leader, Sergio Fajardo, was elected mayor in 2003. The election of Compromiso Ciudadano was momentous: it was the first time a party other than the traditional Liberal or Conservative Parties had been elected, which in itself marked a radical change in the city's political fabric. The party went on to implement the social urbanism agenda, and Mayor Sergio Fajardo has been praised for his 'heroic' vision that is popularly believed to have transformed Medellín.

Compromiso Ciudadano formed as a civic movement during the 1990s as a result of alliances that were forged between academics, activists, NGOs, businesses, and politicians in the fora and seminars associated with the Consejería Presidencial. When its Plan Estratégico para Medellín 1995–1998 was rejected by the city council, it recognised the need for the civic movement to become a formal political party if the policies developed during the 1990s to address the ongoing problems of Medellín's violence were to be implemented. Whilst the focus of discussions of the miracle tends to be the impact of these policies, the politics behind Compromiso Ciudadano – the organisations involved, the way that formal politics changed, and the changes in forms of citizenship, leadership, and power that resulted – has also influenced the place that violence has in the city's politics.

This chapter looks at how Compromiso Ciudadano developed from a social movement to a political party, and the headway it was able to make in Medellín's politics. It examines the development of the party and how its involvement in mainstream politics indicated and created changes in the way that power was acquired and agendas were set in Medellín. A more participatory approach to politics emerged that challenged the populist, clientelist politics and unclear distinction between formal and informal politics and security that had underpinned the prevalence of violence. Furthermore, the forms of leadership and power that emerged during this period represented a change in the values that framed ideas of authority and power and the use of violence as a way to establish authority.

DOI: 10.1057/9781137397362.0010

Compromiso Ciudadano: a reflexive middle class

Members of Compromiso Ciudadano were involved in the committee that drafted the report *Medellín: Reencuentro con el Futuro*, the Seminarios Alternativas para el Futuro, and the working groups that developed the Plan Estratégico. What emerged was, in the words of one member of Compromiso, a 'reflexive middle class'[1] (Betancur et al., 2001). Compromiso Ciudadano 'was able to forge a partnership that defied the traditional political cleavages of the left and right' (Fukuyama and Colby, 2011: 6), and those involved in Compromiso included prominent NGOs such as Corporación Región and the IPC, community associations such as Corporación Convivamos, women's and feminist organisations, academics, and business leaders, as well as politicians, particularly from the emerging 'New Liberal' faction of the Liberal Party (Gutiérrez et al., 2009). The fact that such a coalition could emerge is a testament to how politics in Medellín had changed.

In the context of Colombia's democratic trajectory, the Consejería Presidencial opened up spaces that allowed the articulation of various groups and agendas that changed the political landscape. In the words of academics and activists involved:

> All these years of forums and things, and the Strategic Plan brought together a very diverse group of people into civil society: academics, business people, NGOs, universities. This was a very important process that very few cities have had, but we had it because of the crisis; it was the crisis that brought us to this, to getting together.[2]

> We say that what was established in the city in the nineties, especially between the process of Seminarios Alternativas para el Futuro and the Plan Estratégico was the required reflective environment to set up a proposed solution to the crisis – in economic as well as social terms.[3]

Once this civic movement had become the party Compromiso Ciudadano, it was able to influence formal politics in Medellín to a remarkable extent and challenge the political and economic exclusion that had underpinned much of the violence. However, the limits to its influence, both as a civic movement and later as a political party, are instructive in terms of understanding how violence had been integral to politics in Medellín, how political changes have arguably curtailed this, and why so many problems of violence remain. Although the crisis in violence enabled coalitions to form across a broad political spectrum,

DOI: 10.1057/9781137397362.0010

the organisations involved inevitably had different interpretations of Medellín's problems and different motivations for changing the city. The participation of powerful political and economic organisations enabled the success of Compromiso Ciudadano in implementing its agenda, but it also delimited the possibilities for change.

As discussed in the previous chapter, there were many reasons for businesses to be involved in Compromiso Ciudadano. In particular, the Monitor Group's report and the need for foreign investment spurred businesses to engage with urban regeneration. The discourse of corporate social responsibility was also emerging in the 1990s, and over this period Medellín's business elites were making investments in charitable foundations and university grants for people in marginalised neighbourhoods. The participation of the Sindicato Antioqueño, which at the time controlled around 7 per cent of Colombia's GDP (El Colombiano 2011), was crucial. However, others involved in Compromiso are clear on the importance of these differences in motivation between activists and business participants. One academic characterised the response of Medellín's business leaders thus:

> [They say,] 'We're going to invest there as part of our corporate social responsibility programme to promote the least well off and give them scholarships.' But that does not mean it's out of the goodness of their heart; rather they get reduced taxes, and what's more there are the international issues of 'green manufacturing' ... this means that they are also adapting to these new rules and investing a bit in the environments where they are.[4]

The 'New Liberals' involved in Compromiso Ciudadano were better able to collaborate politically with groups at the more radical end of Medellín's political spectrum than would have been possible for the mainstream Liberal Party. As one sociologist and NGO worker who had been active in Compromiso Ciudadano said:

> In Compromiso Ciudadano you're going to meet these two groups: the people who come from the New Liberalism and the people who come from the left. The New Liberalism was about transparency and anti-narco-traffic, and that's what enabled a coalition with more radical actors, but the New Liberals were not anti-market or pro-democracy in the same way.[5]

In contrast, traditional political elites were conspicuous in their absence from Compromiso Ciudadano. Whilst the city's business and political elites are related in many senses, most notably via the financing of political campaigns, the ways that they exercise power in the city are distinct.

DOI: 10.1057/9781137397362.0010

Whereas the protectionist approach of economic elites sheltered them from direct influence from the cartel, political elites were allegedly more involved with powerful nefarious figures in the city (Carroll, 2011). There are various political reasons for this. One academic involved with Compromiso Ciudadano summarised the situation thus:

> And of these political elites, some of them were strongly permeated by narco-traffic. ... I as a 'legal' politician want to get to the council or the mayor's office, so I'm going to go and look for economic resources from the 'illegal' sector. And the illegal sector looks for a legal politician to be able to protect themselves.[6]

The ways in which formal and informal politicians gained power were very similar. As argued in Chapter 2, the Cartel and other armed groups came to dominate the *comunas* through a populist style of politics – by being the provider of the material goods, shelter, and security that people wanted and needed. This style of leadership was difficult to distinguish from that of more formal politicians, who, because of various institutional factors, including a lack of electoral accountability before the popular election of mayors, also adopted a vertical, gift-giving relationship with the electorate.

The fact that conservatives and politicians who associated with the 'old school' elites in the city were not involved in these processes not only shaped the progress of Compromiso Ciudadano but also limited its agenda. One criticism often levied against social urbanism is that whilst it may have improved the standard of living of many across the city, it has not dealt with issues of justice. The focus has been on infrastructure and modernisation, in accordance with the priorities of the economic elites, which resonated with the agenda of Compromiso and allowed many of its projects to go through. What has changed in this respect, however – in part as a result of the changes in democratic systems outlined in Chapter 4 and the fact that the fora in which Compromiso developed were funded by the national government – is the way that politicians are elected and held to account, and citizens' expectations of their representatives.

Universities and the academy

Medellín-based academics played a prominent role in Compromiso Ciudadano. They were involved in the many reports, consultancies, and seminars of the 1990s, and Mayor Sergio Fajardo and Mayor Alonso Salazar,

DOI: 10.1057/9781137397362.0010

both of whom were leaders of Compromiso Ciudadano, have academic backgrounds. Universities have a curious position in terms of both the establishment of and resistance to elite power. They are at once sites of the reproduction of elite values and expertise, the sites of radical discussion and rebellion and a way to gain the technical knowledge and the cachet needed for upward mobility. In the cartel era and the time of the violence, universities in Medellín, and in Colombia more broadly, were sites of resistance to violent power in the city, corruption, and threats. University professors and students have been murdered on campus in Medellín for their commitment to challenging power in the city. One notorious case is that of Hernan Hanao, a professor of anthropology at the University of Antioquia, who was killed during a faculty meeting, allegedly at the behest of paramilitary leader Carlos Castaño. He had worked on human rights and the displaced in Colombia and at the time was working on the environmental impacts of development in the city (*New York Times*, 1999).

Universities in Medellín have never been ivory towers. There is a history of commitment among academics to the city's development and politics. Individual academics were involved in Compromiso Ciudadano, and some went on to have a role in the Fajardo administration. Fajardo himself has a PhD in maths; Alonso Salazar, Compromiso Ciudadano's second mayor, is a sociologist, and a number of professional architects involved in Compromiso Ciudadano also teach at Medellín's universities. Universities and academics brought with them international networks, particularly networks in Spain, Italy, and the United Kingdom. The National University's Habitat Department was involved in Compromiso Ciudadano from the beginning and has developed a particular participatory approach to urban development in the city. Many civil society organisations have overlapping links with universities, and many prominent actors in community organisations and NGOs also work as academics in universities.

Over this time, the role of universities has changed to include an explicit commitment in their constitution to development in the city according to the national reforms of 1992 – specifically Law 30 (OECD, 2012). For example, the University of EAFIT, as one of its constitutional commitments, has a programme called EAFIT Social, which works with governmental and non-governmental bodies to deliver training programmes and events to promote inclusive development, and one of the main figures associated with social urbanism, Alejandro Echeverri, runs EAFIT's Centre for Urban and Environmental Studies (URBAM).

DOI: 10.1057/9781137397362.0010

Universities have had a prominent role in attracting investment to the city. Whilst departments of social science and the humanities have tended to adopt a critical stance towards modernisation and political developments in Colombia, universities also provide the technically trained workforce that the city's economy requires. The Comité Universidad–Empresa–Estado [University–Firm–State Committee] was established in 2003 with the aim of putting an end to the 'divorce' between business and the academy as well as attracting industry to the city on the basis of appropriate skills and research and development (*El Colombiano*, 2007; OECD, 2012). For example, this committee was involved in bringing the pharmaceutical company Kimberly-Clark to Medellín, and fighting off competition from Bogotá in the process (Hylton, 2007). Once again, there is a coming together of the agenda of attracting investment and the agenda set out by Compromiso Ciudadano, which featured education heavily. However, the effect that this political role has on academic values is questioned. In the words of one academic economist who was particularly sceptical about this process, 'Universities and academics have become nothing but pedlars of certificates and knowledge.'[7]

NGOs, social movements, and community organisations

The NGOs and social movements involved in the Seminarios Alternativas para el Futuro and Compromiso Ciudadano varied along a spectrum from political NGOs that had always tried to engage with formal politics to autonomous NGOs that aimed to change society by creating new political spaces with radically different values. These organisations aligned themselves with autonomous Marxist and feminist perspectives, and they are often associated with the development of Liberation Theology. There are many reasons that the left did not have a political voice in the early 1990s worldwide, but in Colombia progressive political agendas had been silenced for much longer. Many of the people killed in the violent political conflicts throughout the country, and particularly in Medellín, were trade unionists, and Colombia remains the most dangerous country on Earth in which to be engaged in unionism. As one activist from an international NGO explained: 'If you say anything that even remotely hints at redistribution in the States, you're a socialist; if you say it here, you're a terrorist.'[8] The explanation for this is generally held to be the presence of the Marxist guerrilla groups. One senior councillor from the current administration in Medellín who was a former Maoist activist

DOI: 10.1057/9781137397362.0010

made this very clear: 'As long as the FARC exist, the organised left do not have a political future in this country.'[9]

Nevertheless, in the political spaces that opened up during and after the crisis, we do see radical leftist political actors sitting down to discuss policies to address the violence with some of the city's elites. Unlike the trade unions and the cooperative movement, community organisations have continued to gain power throughout the processes of change in Medellín. The violence motivated people to form and join social movements for peace. These were, and continue to be, supported by international human rights organisations, particularly with the NGOisation of development during the 1990s (Carroll, 2011).

The Catholic Church and associated organisations, which have always been central to the construction of elites in Colombia (LaRosa and Mejía, 2012; Restrepo Santamaria, 2011), also had a significant role in the development of social movements and community organisations. The development of Liberation Theology has been associated with the rise of social movements in Latin America. At the centre of Liberation Theology is a Christian commitment to the poor, and adherents to the movement focus on participation and empowerment in their community work, rather than the more vertical relationships created by charity. This approach stands in contrast to the work of Opus Dei, for example, which has been associated with specific elite families in Medellín (Restrepo Santamaria, 2011). Nevertheless, Liberation Theology has a particular place in Medellín's history, as the Conference of Latin American Bishops at which some of the key tenets of Liberation Theology were established, including the Church's emphasis on reducing poverty and critical approach to hierarchy, was held in Medellín in 1968 (Smith, 1991). One of the resolutions of the conference was 'to favour integration, energetically denouncing the abuses and unjust consequences of the excessive inequalities between poor and rich, weak and powerful.'[10]

What was to become one of the most powerful NGOs in Medellín, Corporación Región, was among the first to explicitly and directly engage with formal political power and enter on to the formal political scene in the city. Región's aim is to 'contribute to building and strengthening a broad social and cultural critical consciousness, transforming, with the aim of achieving long-term higher levels of social equity and the radical democratisation of society' (Corporación Región, n.d.; my translation). Región's decision to work with the State marked an important change

DOI: 10.1057/9781137397362.0010

in the city's politics. As one member of the Fajardo administration commented:

> Back then, NGOs took the stance that they would absolutely not engage with the State – the State's over there and we're over here. Región, on the other hand, started the idea that it wasn't like that, that you had to work with the State to be able to get anything done.[11]

The organisation's collaboration with the State included the community fora set up by the Consejería Presidencial to explore and diagnose the problems in the neighbourhoods most affected by the violence. This in turn led to Región's prominence in the Seminarios Alternativas para el Futuro and its participation in various working groups. Like Salazar, Clara Restrepo, who was also in Región, went on to be in Fajardo's cabinet.

Community organisations, such as Corporación Convivamos,[12] were also able to gain traction in the wake of the crisis. Corporación Convivamos was formed in 1990 in the northeast zone of the city. Still in existence, its aims are to promote local development via education, community support, and participatory action research. The organisation has its roots in Liberation Theology and the Cuban revolution. Although it was officially formed in the 1990s, the group of people who established this organisation were already active in the community: 'We played football together,' remembered one of the leaders. 'Football was one of the ways that you could group together in public without being suspected of being in the militia or some gang.'[13] As a community organisation, Convivamos was not a threat to economic power in the way a trade union could be perceived to be.

One of the leaders of Convivamos, who had been involved since its inception, traced the changing dynamic between this community organisation and the State: 'We used to be a kind of charity case – left to the "Gray Ladies" [women who volunteered for charity organisations].'[14] With the Consejería Presidencial and the fora that it opened, Convivamos had direct involvement in implementing projects that were part of the Plan Estratégico para Medellín 1995–1998. There is, however, a fear that community organisations such as Convivamos have left behind their political commitments and are working within frameworks that no longer provide them with the latitude for participation to be meaningful.

Many women's organisations in Medellín and nationally formed to protest the violence and to campaign for peace (Murdock, 2008). There are also organisations that campaign for the rights of women specifically,

DOI: 10.1057/9781137397362.0010

for a recognition of violence within the home as part of the broader spectrum of conflict in Colombia and Medellín, and for women's economic rights and education. These organisations are inherently critical of the status quo in Medellín and the elite structures that have dominated society. Unlike leftist organisations, they are not directly associated with the Marxist discourses of the FARC. Women's organisations and organisations adopting an explicitly critical, feminist agenda also found space within formal politics in the 1990s and 2000s in Medellín. That such radical agendas obtained a political voice within formal political settings illustrates the extent of the political changes that emerged after the crisis.

Women's movements in Medellín were able to gain power within formal politics, via the processes and spaces that opened up in the city over the 1990s, and, on this basis, develop projects predicated on a feminist approach to development within the local government apparatus. Women's organisations included movements for peace in Colombia and Medellín specifically, including such groups as Ruta Pacífica de la Mujer [Women's Peaceful Path], Vamos Mujer [Women, Let's Go], and Mujeres que Crean [Creative Women]. Feminist activists were also involved in the campaign for women's reproductive rights, and some were forced into exile because of the risks involved in taking part in this campaign. As with other organisations in Colombia, there is a continuing distinction between those groups that identify as autonomous and those 'political' organisations willing to work with the State, but there is a distinct feminist presence in mainstream approaches to development in the city that has grown with the social urbanism agenda.

Among the working groups that developed out of the Seminarios Alternativas para el Futuro was the Working Group for Women, the mechanism via which local government could consult with community women's organisations. In collaboration with other working groups on related themes such as livelihoods, sustainability, and family well-being, the Working Group for Women was able to establish lasting relations with local administrations (Gobernación de Antioquia, 2003). This group is consulted on issues of economic development, as well as issues of gender equality more narrowly defined. In addition to participating directly, established women's organisations provided training to community women's organisations on how to participate in the working group, present their agenda, and, crucially, monitor and follow up on agreements (*El Colombiano*, 2013a).

DOI: 10.1057/9781137397362.0010

With the establishment of the Sub-Secretariat for Women in the municipal government in 2002, the women's movement gained a foothold in formal government. Sergio Fajardo's partner, Lucrecia Ramírez-Restrepo, herself an active feminist, was instrumental in promoting and lobbying for a body dedicated to gender equality within local government. One high-profile element of this campaign was to replace the town hall-sponsored beauty contest with an annual competition for 'Young Women with Talent' in which prizes are given for poetry, art, science, and enterprise (Concejo de Medellín, 2007). As a result of the successful establishment of the sub-secretariat, a number of feminist programmes have been developed that influence two of the key themes of social urbanism: solidarity economy and education.

Worldwide, there are programmes that target women and girls with the aim of promoting development, rather than on the basis of women's rights. Microfinance programmes and high-profile education campaigns cite the benefits of targeting women because of the positive development impacts that this can yield. Examples of feminist programmes that problematise the assumptions about women's roles implicit in more mainstream interventions and prioritise women's empowerment over correlated benefits for development are rarer. Nevertheless, although, as illustrated in the previous chapter, the policies adopted to promote education and solidarity economy in the *comunas* are motivated as much by the needs of international business as by the desire to address exclusion and inequality, under these rubrics more critical programmes, including feminist programmes, have found a space.

The approach to economic development espoused by the sub-secretariat is to define the barriers women face in accessing the economy on their own terms, to problematise assumptions behind what is valued in the economy while recognising women's work, and to challenge naturalised assumptions about why women should, typically, be carrying out reproductive labour. In Medellín, the idea that women should exclusively perform reproductive labour is strongly reinforced in mainstream society, most notably in analyses concluding that the cause of the violence was the breakdown of traditional family structures. Women in the *comunas* of Medellín face challenges which come from being in a city where so many citizens have been victims of displacement from rural areas, where the rate of intra-urban displacement is the highest in the world, and where the majority of displaced persons are women and children (*Personería de Medellín*, 2011).

DOI: 10.1057/9781137397362.0010

The idea of solidarity economy, which has been a key slogan associated with Medellín's transformation and has a place in the Colombian Constitution of 1991, has provided a platform from which programmes that reflect feminist analyses of economic exclusion can be implemented. The livelihoods activities run from the sub-secretariat have used the policies promoting community associations and the participatory budget to encourage women's participation in political debate, encouraging the formation of associations not only to tender for public contracts but also to form a political identity as community women. This has particular importance given the isolation often experienced by women in the *comunas* as a result of the breakdown of community ties associated with violence and displacement and the way that industrialisation incorporated women as home workers. The sub-secretariat is involved in training programmes on group formation and management, in addition to training community women to conduct a needs assessment of their own area and design projects that best meet those needs. The associations established via this process include groups working on teaching, child care, tourism, and catering.

The distinctiveness of the sub-secretariat's approach comes from the process via which these associations are built. The aim, unlike in mainstream interventions that target women, is that women's position and gender equality be improved by the creation of these associations, rather than the associations being an end in themselves. The training given includes advocacy and campaigning for women's rights within the communities and continued accompaniment, despite the general requirement that such activities promptly achieve 'sustainability'. Such interventions and approaches have a history in feminist activism and in some women's NGOs. The surprising element of these interventions in Medellín is that they have found a place in the city government.

One of the main themes that brought together businesses, politicians, and progressive political agendas in Medellín in the 1990s was education. The Monitor Group's report referred explicitly to the importance of mass education to the development of a service economy. Many of the NGOs involved in the discussions after the crisis, as well as Compromiso Ciudadano, also prioritised education and included it as an explicit part of their mission. However, perspectives on education can differ enormously. Whilst economists tend to see education as creating human capital that can improve economic performance at various levels, there is a tradition of popular education in Latin America that is strongly

DOI: 10.1057/9781137397362.0010

influenced by Liberation Theology and the work of Paolo Freire. Popular education is premised on the notion that, rather than recreating and reinforcing political structures, education should provide a platform from which students can gain a critical stance on their own position, from a perspective grounded in their own experiences and worldviews. Rather than seeing teaching as the transmission of information, popular education classes are frequently participatory, creating a dialectic relationship between teacher and students. This approach stands in contrast to colonial approaches to education, which involve the imposition of the coloniser's language, religion, and worldviews, but it can also be contrasted with human capital approaches to learning, which define education as a transfer of skills rather than a development of critical understanding.

The training programmes run by the sub-secretariat, in alliance with the Escuela Normal Superior de Medellín [Medellín Higher Teacher Training College], adopt a popular education approach. The training is formal, in that students receive a teaching diploma enabling them to enter the job market, but also explicitly validates the skills and knowledge that students already have. Teaching alternates between theory in the classroom and the practice of care work and education in the home. Theory informs and develops caring and education practices that students perform in their everyday lives, whilst the practice of care work is also a platform from which to critique dominant ideas of education. As one student commented, 'We learn about those ideas from sociology and economics and that, but those disciplinary divisions don't reflect the reality of our lives – we're expert in that.'[15] At the same time, the students use class discussions to develop an analytical framework for the difficulties they have had to overcome to attend the class, including threats from family members who think that a woman should be in the home, extortion, intra-urban displacement, and even kidnapping.

Other organisations that adopt this approach include the IPC, which 'is part of the tradition of critical thinking in Latin America that emphasise the importance of inclusion, and aims to develop education and research programmes that create social transformation' (IPC, n.d.). The IPC, along with Región, was a central actor in the development of the Seminarios Alternativas para el Futuro and Compromiso Ciudadano, and it continues to maintain a critical perspective whilst working with the State. The IPC's involvement, as an established, critical organisation, exemplifies the political process that would not have been possible before

DOI: 10.1057/9781137397362.0010

the political changes of the early 1990s or the crisis of violence. The participation of the IPC in training, conflict resolution, and research in the *comunas* in turn led to the establishment of other community organisations. As one IPC member who had been involved in such programmes said, 'These people had always been very absent from the work of the State. So, when various organisations arrived to do a project for them, it was very significant.'[16] As a result of such training, community members took part in some of the principal working groups that influenced the various development plans that came to form social urbanism. The IPC was also involved in the working groups on participation and employment, conducting research with community organisations to ground these ideas in the local environment and to support the formation of cooperatives on the basis of their research.

The formation of Compromiso Ciudadano was hence remarkable in bringing together organisations from diverse perspectives, and developing spaces which included programmes that were critical of the status quo but yet had the support of mainstream business and political leaders. The alliance of these interests was necessary from a pragmatic point of view to be able to implement the social urbanism agenda, but also represents a change in the city's politics. This did not happen in isolation, as we saw in Chapter 4, and many are concerned that the continued adherence to a bottom line of economic competitiveness may undermine progressive social developments, despite the aim to unify 'competitiveness and solidarity' in the city's slogan. Nevertheless, the political space made in the wake of the crisis allowed progressive, even radical organisations to influence the formal political agenda, and go some way to addressing the exclusion that for many underpinned such high levels of violence.

Different kinds of citizen: participation and critique

One key aspect of how violence entered Medellín's political landscape was the political culture of the city: the elite dominance of formal politics and the populist approach to garnering votes. As a 'reflexive middle class', the members of Compromiso Ciudadano did not represent the city's elite and in themselves posed a challenge to Medellín's political formations. By being made up of the representatives of social movements, civil society, businesses, and universities, but backed by the national and international power that had been invested in the Consejería Presidencial

DOI: 10.1057/9781137397362.0010

and the Seminarios Alternativas para el Futuro, they were well placed to challenge the city's power structures. The participation of organisations such as Región, Convivamos, feminist movements, and the IPC alongside representatives from business, such as Pro-Antioquia, and the political class in the form of the New Liberals changed political process in the city, albeit temporarily. It is not possible to link this directly to the decline in violence, but in terms of the diagnoses made by these very actors, the processes behind the Medellín Miracle had already begun to challenge the political and social exclusion that had enabled the violence before social urbanism was implemented.

Whilst the discourses of the 'historical social debt' and 'changing the skin of the city' indicated that exclusion and inequality were the underlying problems, participation of these distinct and opposed groups in the fora of the 1990s, within the context of constitutional and electoral change, disrupted the way that spaces created by inequality and exclusion could be exploited. Bringing erstwhile radical organisations into the folds of the State, albeit within certain parameters, changed the attitudes involved in interactions between citizen and State. The clientelism that had characterised formal politicians, as well as the activities of Escobar, may have begun to change during the 1990s.

The emphasis on participation allowed different people to be involved in setting the agenda, and it also challenged the nature of leadership, which had tended to be more along the lines of a *caudillo*-style, individualist, vertical structure. The more horizontal structure necessitated by participatory leadership was itself a challenge to the paternalist, vertical style of leadership which had been a factor in allowing violent actors to gain power. From the point of view of policymakers, the project has been about changing the political subject:

> It's about making suggestions, not just demands. We have a history of populism in this city and that has been a cause of the violence, the *caudillo*-style leadership and the exclusion. The participatory budget and the educational programmes are about creating a different kind of political subject – not just one that makes demands on their own behalf, but one that makes suggestions.[17]

However, from the perspective of community members, these developments have depended as much on changes in political norms and the attitude of formal powers as on training and participation:

> There is a system of community networks and citizen leadership, and there's respect for that, a recognition, which leads to empowerment. Now, you can

DOI: 10.1057/9781137397362.0010

participate in a community assembly and they're not going to crush you and say that what you're saying is useless.[18]

Advances in the accessibility of formal political spaces depend as much on the provision made for participation in the 1991 Constitution as on specific developments in Medellín. Nevertheless, the education and community programmes outlined above have provided a framework within which to critique and react to abuses of power. As two community leaders commentated:

> What happens is that throughout the city you need a *padrino* [patron], the guy who's going to help you out... but if you don't know anyone who'll do that it's difficult.... But it should not be like that because some things are constitutional rights.[19]

> What we've learnt is that you've got to make a fuss so that the State does what it's meant to for us.[20]

The participatory budget, although not without drawbacks, also altered the dynamics between community activism and formal political representation.

> When a community had to go to a councillor and ask for his help just to get a bit of money to build a park, or the pavements, a school room, and all that. Then, what happened was that [with the participatory budget] the mediation that had been necessary was broken. Traditional politicians don't like the participatory budget because it took away their power to manipulate leaders, because it used to be that leaders would work for them in exchange for votes. You get that work done for me, I'll get you the votes.... This was a radical rupture.[21]

Despite these developments, participation remains delimited by 'technical' considerations that often reflect the economic demands of the city rather than the political and social demands of the communities. As one professional architect who was in Fajardo's administration put it:

> Of course we arrived [saying] this is what we want, but it was then subject to participation. With the Development Plan, we swept across the city, we worked with leaders, with the communities, and we collected and systematised all of the proposals of the leaders. Obviously this did not radically change the Development Plan, but adjustments were made.... What we had was the technical part, but it had been participatory, enriched by the community.[22]

When Compromiso Ciudadano became a political party and chose Sergio Fajardo as its leader, more technical forms of governance were at the heart of its approach to development in the city, social urbanism, and countering the violence. This approach represented a radical change from the clientelist, indeed corrupt, political powers that had characterised the city, but presents challenges when considering the limits of meaningful participation and the exclusion that can be created by modernisation projects run on purely technical lines. Nevertheless, the development of more technical approaches to governance is part of broader changes in political culture in Medellín.

Cultures of power

A key moment in Compromiso Ciudadano's history was when it decided to put forward a candidate for political office. Until 1999, Compromiso Ciudadano was a horizontally structured organisation that identified as a civil rather than political movement. There was, however, a realisation, when its Plan Estratégico was rejected by the City Council, that to take real power and make real change it would have to take a more active role in formal politics. The decision to become a political party and enter the mayoral elections necessitated finding a leader. The deliberations around the choice of that leader, and the characteristics which subsequent leaders embodied, demonstrate how the face of power – which had been associated with '*tumbao* culture' and the 'macho' Pablo Escobar, as well as the exploitative, vertical relationships established by traditional politicians – had begun to change. New political forces that used the spaces that emerged during the 1990s had very different visions of power and leadership. Although violence remains present in the configuration of relations of power, Medellín's transformation over the last 20 years – underpinned by changes in political structures – has changed the nature of leadership, authority, and legitimacy in the city.

Sergio Fajardo is often a central focus of media attention on the Medellín Miracle, but in the words of one Compromiso insider, 'he got to be mayor in my opinion as a result of the processes of the last 10 or 12 years'.[23] The process of choosing a leader was complex, and the movement explicitly looked for someone outside its membership and outside traditional politics, but with the political clout within the city and the connections to be effective. These criteria demonstrate the balance that is often necessary in political change and characterises the tensions inherent in bringing out change from a crisis. Although

DOI: 10.1057/9781137397362.0010

the crisis generated more room for radical political voices to emerge, the structures and institutions that upheld traditional power in the city were still in existence.

Several political leaders who could achieve this balance were considered by the members of Compromiso Ciudadano. The criteria for choosing Sergio Fajardo as a candidate for mayor of Medellín demonstrated the importance of a political understanding of Medellín in the movement's success. As one member of Compromiso Ciudadano said, 'He's a man who can move among the elites and is also capable of connecting with people in the communities.'[24] He had worked with the city's leaders, including Alvaro Uribe, the governor of Antioquia at that time and a central figure in Medellín's political elite. He had the appropriate background, coming from an upper-class family and having been educated in the United States, where he obtained his PhD from the University of Wisconsin. However, it was judged that he was also enough of an outsider, as an academic and a resident of Bogotá, to bring a new element to formal politics. After he was identified by Compromiso Ciudadano as a possible candidate, he further immersed himself in the city's political scene by working for a year as a journalist at the influential Medellín-based newspaper *El Colombiano*.

Fajardo had the appropriate elite cultural capital and networks to be accepted as a leader. However, he and the subsequent mayor, Alonso Salazar, were characterised as 'illustrious outsiders' whose election was seen as 'a slap in the face for the political parties that had historically wielded power' (Barcelona Metropolis, 2010). Fajardo's administration in some ways represented a challenge to the powers-that-be, but it has also been alleged that Fajardo's election was the elites' way of 'putting in one of their own'.[25] The people he chose to work with him were 'trusted people' – people he had known at university, for example, and who had elite careers but were outside the realm of politics. They campaigned by 'putting on their sandals',[26] going out into the *barrios*, and appealing to the more democratic potential of popular mayoral elections. At the same time, many argued that the city's traditional power-brokers had simply marshalled 'a group of twelve shining knights from the elite'[27] to form a government – indicating that the balance between the continuity of power structures and more progressive politics may be a marriage of convenience.

Salazar's mayoralty can be usefully contrasted with Fajardo's in terms of the balance between change and continuity involved in the political

DOI: 10.1057/9781137397362.0010

processes behind the Medellín Miracle. Whereas Fajardo was from an elite background, Salazar was from a middle-class family. Salazar prioritised the issues of justice and corruption, and his success was much more limited. In one tale told about Salazar as mayor, he had become so frustrated at the apparent imperviousness of the authorities to corruption and abuses of power, and especially at the refusal to arrest one particular repeat offender, that he went round with his driver and arrested the man himself. This shows the limits of social urbanism, which is criticised for making limited progress on issues of reparative and retributive justice, even if it raises standards of living via its modernisation projects. Whilst the modernisation processes have the blessing of a broad range of people, including certain factions among the elites, justice issues bring out long-running problems that continue to create tensions and violence.

The election of Compromiso Ciudadano and the way their approach is explained by members of the Fajardo administration exemplify a move towards more 'rational/technical' leadership. As a mathematician, Fajardo was known for using clear numerical justifications for his policies. The decisions on where to focus architectural projects and investment in education were based entirely on development indicators. In response to my question about how Fajardo was able to persuade such a range of people to invest in these areas, one former member of his government said: 'Fajardo did not negotiate. Never. He had the figures, he didn't need to. If people objected he would present the numbers as a technical issue.'[28] Compared with the traditional leadership style of the patrimonial elites in the city, the fact that Fajardo was able to gain authority through his technical expertise indicates the change that the coalition behind his leadership meant for political culture and leadership in the city.

As a further illustration of this shift towards a more rational, technical form of leadership, the Fajardo administration based its interventions on Human Development Index data – the areas with the lowest development indicators were the ones that received investment, representing what was perceived to be a radical change:

> In the Medellín council, they were used to thinking, 'I represent this community, they have a project to carry out and as long as I have the votes to be re-elected, I'll help with the proposal.' ... But we would develop a government programme, and we'd put it on the table, and Sergio would say, 'That's where the city has most need,' and we even favoured a great majority of the population who never voted for us, so we weren't paying them back for votes, but rather we were doing what was technically correct, what should be done.[29]

This also was seen as causing a tension with the political class and representing a change in the way that people gain power:

> The whole of the political class, literally, who had interests in Medellín ended up becoming to a certain degree opposed to our administration, because we had become a danger politically speaking, above all for corrupt politicians of course. ... Finally, society is complaining about corrupt politicians. ... And of course it's poverty, corruption and egoism which put corrupt leaders in power.[30]

A crucial mechanism that enabled Compromiso to become a successful political party was the popular election of mayors, which structured changes in the political class. It is also clear that without the development of Compromiso Ciudadano over the previous ten years, Fajardo would not have become mayor. It is, however, Fajardo who has taken centre stage in discussions of social urbanism and Medellín's 'miraculous' transformation. He is frequently called a 'visionary' and is the basis for some claims that 'development needs heroes' (Fajardo and Andrews, 2014). This attenuates the potential that Compromiso Ciudadano, as a horizontal organisation that involved the participation of various actors and developed without a leader, could be making. Sergio Fajardo is known for his charisma and wit (Devlin and Chaskel, 2010), and members of his administration refer to the energy that was created around him and the sense, particularly at the beginning of his administration, that this government was really going to change something:

> It was incredible to work with him – the speed at which ideas came out of the meetings that we had, and really creative discourses that really caught on. 'Social urbanism' is an obvious example, but he came up with them at a rate of knots.[31]

Whilst the focus on Fajardo is understandable, the heroism with which he has become associated represents the continuation of individualistic, vertical ideas of authority that were part of the culture that framed the rise to power of authoritarian, *caudillo*, and violent actors.

Women's organisations and the Sub-Secretariat for Women have been prominent in policymaking in the city, as we have seen, and their participation has changed the style of leadership that is recognised as authoritative. Without adopting essentialist ideas of femininity and peace, it can be argued that women are under less pressure to conform to competitive and indeed aggressive styles of leadership and authority, and do not lose face when adopting a more collaborative approach (Kronsell

DOI: 10.1057/9781137397362.0010

and Svedberg, 2011). The actions of men, on the other hand, are judged in terms of their conformity to hegemonic masculinity – culturally situated constructions of the type of man who can become 'the alpha male'. In the context of decades of violence and renowned 'macho' constructions of male power in Colombia, the fact that women have had a prominent place in Medellín's recent history itself marks a change in the gender – in terms of both masculinity and femininity – of power there.

It has been observed that women's role in formal politics and peace negotiations in Colombia is limited (Rojas et al., 2004; Alvarez, 2009). However, in addition to the involvement of women's and feminist organisations in the processes of the 1990s, several women have been prominent in high-ranking positions in Medellín's formal political apparatus. For example, the head of the Consejería Presidencial, Maria Emma Mejía, was nominated to that role after being President Gaviria's chief of campaigns during the election. It was generally considered a surprise that she was given this post, because 'it looked like he'd left a society girl in the middle of a breeding ground for hired guns' (*Semana*, 1993). A number of women emphasised that men in Medellín 'hated women with power' and that they had been judged harshly as women who worked rather than dedicating themselves to children – either by not having any or by leaving them in child care while they worked. There was also a perception that some women, once in positions of power, 'opt to mimic a typically masculine kind of leadership'.[32] Nevertheless, the individualistic, brutal style of leadership that was characteristic of and, arguably, a causal factor in the violence was challenged by an expanded role for the women's movement in formal politics. As one activist put it, 'If it wasn't for the women's movement, we'd have ended up with the same machos as before'.[33]

Conclusion

Compromiso Ciudadano was at once the result of changes in the political landscape in Medellín and the body that effected change in the city – not only with its policies but also via the way the party constructed and exercised power. Compromiso Ciudadano has its roots in the participatory process of the Consejería Presidencial during the 1990s, and it is characterised by a remarkable breadth of participation, both within the fora in which the policies of social urbanism were developed and

DOI: 10.1057/9781137397362.0010

in the projects that it implemented. This changed ideas of citizenship, power, and authority and the long-running political dynamics that had been diagnosed as underpinning the violence. Compromiso Ciudadano successfully achieved many of its aims, but in its choice of leader and in the policies it was able to get through, the limitations of these changes are clear. The policies that were enacted tended to resonate with the concerns of traditional powers, with whom compromise needed to be reached.

It is recognised by many in the city and in Fajardo's administration that whilst the standard of living, in particular in marginalised areas, has improved, the political system, and the structures within which politics is performed in Medellín, to a large extent remain unchanged:

> In the end, I think that this has been like a cruise ship that's going in one direction, and the inertia of the history of this city, of the culture of this city, is such that you can only manage to change its direction a little. ... We achieved very important things, but we did not manage to transform the city.[34]

The limits of the 'miracle' are important to acknowledge, in particular the outstanding issues of justice which social urbanism does not address. Nevertheless, Compromiso Ciudadano represents developing political processes in Medellín that in themselves address some of the reasons Medellín became such a violent place. The exclusivity of political elites and the protectionism of entrepreneurial elites were, for a time, attenuated as groups which had been considered beyond the pale attained a seat at the table. In addition to the re-focusing of urban regeneration policies which this facilitated, it began to change approaches to citizenship, and different expectations of political leaders developed that challenged the vertical, populist dynamics associated with the rise to power of violent leaders. Similarly, the technical approach adopted to urban regeneration may have begun to displace the prominence of violence in political processes.

Notes

1   Academic and NGO activist, interview, 7 August 2012.
2   NGO activist, interview, 7 August 2012.
3   Human rights activist, interview, 6 August 2012.
4   Academic, interview, 5 August 2012.
5   NGO activist, interview, 7 August 2012.

DOI: 10.1057/9781137397362.0010

6   Academic, interview, 5 August 2012.

7   Academic, interview, 2 August 2012.

8   Informal communication, March 2012.

9   Councillor, interview, 1 August 2012.

10   Schalbach, Gerald (n.d.) Medellín 1968 (excerpts), Conference of Latin American Bishops, Medellín, Colombia. Available at: http://www.geraldschlabach.net/Medellin-1968-excerpts/

11   Member of the Fajardo administration, interview, 8 August 2012.

12   The 'Let's Live Together' Corporation. This organisation preceded the creation of the paramilitary/private security organisations Las CONVIVR referred to in Chapter 2. As a result of the creation of these groups, the community organisation changed its name from Corporación Convivir to Corporación Convivamos, to clarify that there was no connection.

13   NGO activist, interview, 23 July 2012.

14   NGO activist, interview, 23 July 2012.

15   Focus group, Escuela Normal Superior de Medellín, 19 October 2011.

16   Academic and NGO activist, interview, 7 August 2012.

17   Focus group, Sub-Secretariat for Participation, 17 July 2012.

18   Focus group of community leaders, 24 July 2012.

19   Focus group of community leaders, 24 July 2012.

20   Focus group of community leaders, 24 July 2012.

21   Member of the Fajardo administration, interview, 8 August 2012.

22   Member of the Fajardo administration, interview, 17 July 2012.

23   NGO activist, interview, 7 August 2012.

24   Member of the Fajardo administration, interview, 8 August 2012.

25   Medellín councillor, interview, 16 July 2012.

26   Member of the Fajardo administration, interview, 24 July 2012.

27   Cultural worker, interview, 30 July 2012.

28   Member of the Fajardo administration, interview, 17 July 2012.

29   Member of the Fajardo administration, interview, 8 August 2012.

30   Member of the Fajardo administration, interview, 17 July 2012.

31   Member of the Fajardo administration, interview, 8 August 2012.

32   Feminist activist, interview, 26 July 2012.

33   NGO activist, interview, 15 December 2012.

34   Member of the Fajardo administration, interview, 17 July 2012.

DOI: 10.1057/9781137397362.0010

Conclusion

Abstract: *The conclusion reflects on the policies, discourses, and politics of the Medellín Miracle, asking how these political processes could have been related to the dramatic decline in violence. It is argued that the distinctive elements of the Medellín Miracle, which distinguish social urbanism from other international models of urban development, are the political changes that accompanied these policies. The broader significance of the Medellín case is that, if epidemic violence is understood as a question of how power is attained, wielded, and maintained in a certain context, then changes in political processes are as much a factor in the reduction of violence as the iconic buildings and infrastructure projects that have come to symbolise the 'miracle'.*

Keywords: Medellín miracle; politics of violence

Maclean, Kate. *Social Urbanism and the Politics of Violence: The Medellín Miracle*. Basingstoke: Palgrave Macmillan, 2015. DOI: 10.1057/9781137397362.0011.

In 2013, Medellín was awarded the Urban Land Institute's prize for Most Innovative City. The award focused on the infrastructural developments in the city, which were perceived to have contributed to the rapid decline in violence:

> Few cities have transformed the way that Medellín ... has in the past 20 years. The city built public libraries, parks, and schools in poor hillside neighbourhoods and constructed a series of transportation links from there to its commercial and industrial centres. (*Wall Street Journal*, 2013)

The summary of the institute's reasons for giving the award to Medellín goes on to specify the importance of the politics behind the change, emphasising that 'a change in the institutional fabric of the city may be as important' as the tangible infrastructure projects' (*Wall Street Journal*, 2013).

The reasons for giving Medellín this prize reflect feelings within the city, which are predominantly that politics and process are more important than the new buildings and structures themselves. This book has detailed these institutional changes and clarified the importance of Colombia's trajectory towards democracy and accompanying constitutional and electoral changes, as well as the changes in Medellín's political landscape after the crisis of violence was recognised in the early 1990s. Crucially, the agendas of progressive social movements coincided with policy recommendations for attracting foreign direct investment. The discourses framing the fora and discussions of the 1990s allowed room for the policies recommended to appeal to elites' sense of stewardship, at the same time as facilitating a progressive redistribution of power and the creation of a more inclusive economy. Compromiso Ciudadano and its social urbanism agenda were effective precisely because of the balance achieved, politically and discursively, between challenging the powers-that-be and appealing to elite tastes, priorities, and economic interests.

Despite the success in terms of implementing the social urbanism agenda, there is concern that the consensus found between an inclusive, progressive agenda and the needs of global capital is once more becoming dominated by elite concerns. There continue to be problems of extreme violence, displacement, disenfranchisement, inequality, and poverty in the *comunas* of Medellín, and the worry is that now the city has been successfully rebranded, the *comunas* are once again being forgotten. The fact that the award for Most Innovative City was sponsored by Citibank has been extremely controversial and sheds light on the fragility of the

DOI: 10.1057/9781137397362.0011

political coalitions that were achieved during the 1990s. In response to the celebrations at the receipt of the award, the Archbishop of Medellín, in an article in the Medellín-based Newspaper *El Colombiano*, reminded his fellow citizens that Medellín continues to be the most violent city in the country and that many questions around justice, narco-traffic, and continued violence remain unanswered (*El Colombiano*, 2013b). Similarly, the IPC issued a press statement in which it highlighted that another report to be released that week, on human rights in Medellín, was less complimentary and 'revealed much about a reality which cannot be hidden, despite the efforts to make over an image to sell to foreigners, which is not believable for those who daily see themselves impeded from their right to move by barriers that are getting bigger and bigger' (IPC, 2013).

It is impossible to isolate discrete factors that caused the reduction in Medellín's violence. In fact, the whole tenor of this book has been to problematise the idea that there are technical solutions to violence, or to development more broadly. Although there is an awareness of the importance of political process and institutional change in the city's apparent transformation, the emergence of the Medellín 'model' of urban regeneration in the context of high levels of violence suggests that specific policies are being exported to other violence-plagued areas as a 'technical fix'. The technical fixes proposed – infrastructure, iconic architecture, public spaces – bear a striking resemblance to those adopted by many other second-tier cities across the world. Although they have been adapted and added to in the specific Medellín context – most notably in the importance given to participation, the development of community groups, and economic inclusion – it is unclear that they have represented a real challenge to the shape that the city would have taken were it simply to have obeyed the needs of capital. The needs of capital will, on occasion, coincide with the needs of excluded populations and challenge the control of traditional elites, but this is a very different approach to urban design from that espoused by advocates of 'a right to the city' and cannot be trusted to maintain an inclusive agenda in the long term.

There is hence reason to be sceptical about the Medellín Miracle. It is being widely praised on the international stage – and many more reports have come out about the success of the Medellín model since the city hosted the World Urban Forum in April 2014, including one by Nobel Prize winner Joseph Stiglitz (*Guardian*, 2014). But few of these glowing reports – often written from a progressive perspective by people who

DOI: 10.1057/9781137397362.0011

want to believe that investing in inclusion, libraries, and public spaces can heal violence-ridden cities – mention the State violence that pacified the *comunas* in 2002, just before these policies were implemented. Nor do they mention the negotiations with paramilitaries at the international level and the alleged complicity of Medellín paramilitary groups in pacifying *comunas*.

Nevertheless, it would be doing a disservice to the social movements, community groups, women's movements, NGOs, and university academics who were involved in the development of Compromiso Ciudadano and the social urbanism agenda to put the decline in violence entirely down to the broader factors of the needs of capital and Uribe's 'iron fist'. The political spaces that emerged in the wake of the peak of the city's violence and the Consejería Presidencial needed to be 'worked'. The fact that Corporación Región, the IPC, Corporación Convivamos, and the Sub-Secretariat for Women could be established and gain power represents a remarkable change in the city's power structures. The developing participatory approaches to governance have the potential – although, again, there are fears that the current political momentum is going against this – to disrupt and challenge clientelist, *caudillo* styles of leadership that ensure that violence has a place in political process, as much as any macroeconomic and political factors. That these organisations continue to have a voice in setting the agenda is as remarkable as the iconic library and Metrocable.

The broader lesson from the Medellín Miracle is that the solutions to violence, just like its causes, need to be understood in context. Architectural and technical solutions to urban violence are not the causes of change but the manifestation of underlying changes in the complex political, cultural, and economic processes that foment endemic violence.

DOI: 10.1057/9781137397362.0011

References

Abadinsky, H. (2009) *Organized crime.* Wadsworth, CA: Cengage Learning.

Alcaldía de Medellín (1996) *Programa Integral de Mejoramiento de Barrios Subnormales – PRIMED: Una experiencia exitosa en la intervención urbana.* Available at: http://unesdoc.unesco.org/ images/0012/001297/129776so.pdf (accessed June 2014).

Alvarez, J. E. (2009) Doing gender in the midst of war: The example of the demobilization process of paramilitaries in Medellin, Colombia 2003–2007. *Peace Studies Journal* 2(2): 51–76.

Amnesty International (2005) *Colombia: Justice and peace law will guarantee impunity for human rights abusers.* Available at: http://www.amnesty.org/en/library/info/ AMR23/012/2005 (accessed June 2014).

Amnesty International (2011) *Colombia: Hidden from justice impunity for conflict-related sexual violence. A follow-up report.* Available at: http://www.amnestyusa. org/sites/default/files/colombia_vaw_report_oct._4_ embargoed.pdf (accessed June 2014).

APN (1990) Government extradites two accused drug smugglers to U.S. Available at: http://www. apnewsarchive.com/1990/Government-Extradites-Two-Accused-Drug-Smugglers-To-U-S-/ id-fd1909ae1cbde4a10077a38eac681bf3 (accessed June 2014).

Arbeláez, M., Echavarría, J., Gaviria, A., & Vélez, C. (2001) *Colombian long run growth and the crisis of the 1990s.* Global Development Network/Inter-American

Development Bank. Available at: http://lacea.org/WEB/country_ studies/colombia.pdf (accessed June 2014).

Arendt, H. (1970) *On violence*. Boston, MA: Houghton Mifflin Harcourt.

Atkinson, R. (2003) Domestication by cappuccino or a revenge on urban space? Control and empowerment in the management of public spaces. *Urban Studies* 40(9): 1829–1843.

Atkinson, R. (2006) Padding the bunker: Strategies of middle-class disaffiliation and colonisation in the city. *Urban Studies* 43(4): 819–832.

Auyero, J. (2000) The logic of clientelism in Argentina: An ethnographic account. *Latin American Research Review* 35(3): 55–81.

Avilés, W. (2006) Paramilitarism and Colombia's low-intensity democracy. *Journal of Latin American Studies* 38(2): 379–408.

Barcelona Metropolis (2010) *Urbanismo social: La metamorfosis de Medellín.* Available at: http://w2.bcn.cat/bcnmetropolis/arxiu/es/ page6dde.html?id=21&ui=331&prevNode=33&tagId=23 (accessed June 2014).

Bateman, M., J. P. D., Ortíz, & Maclean, K. (2011) *A post-Washington consensus approach to local economic development in Latin America? An example from Medellín, Colombia.* ODI Background Note. Available at: http://www.odi.org.uk/sites/odi.org.uk/files/odi-assets/publications-opinion-files/7054.pdf (accessed June 2014).

BBC (2010) *Remarkable renewal brings visitors to Medellín.* Available at: http://news.bbc.co.uk/1/hi/programmes/fast_track/8850289.stm (accessed June 2014).

BBC (2012) *Pink Cardiff street lights plan 'to deter ASBO yobs'.* Available at: http://www.bbc.co.uk/news/uk-wales-17260959 (accessed June 2014).

BBC (2013) *Colombia's armed groups.* Available at: http://www.bbc.co.uk/ news/world-latin-america-11400950 (accessed June 2014).

BBC (2014) *Colombia election: Santos to face Zuluaga in run-off.* Available at: http://www.bbc.co.uk/news/world-latin-america-27567604 (accessed June 2014).

Bejarano, A. M., & Pizarro Leongómez, E. (2002) *From 'restricted' to 'besieged': The changing nature of the limits to democracy in Colombia.* Working Paper 296. Available at: http://kellogg.nd.edu/publications/ workingpapers/WPS/296.pdf (accessed June 2014).

Bernal-Franco, L., & Navas-Caputo, C. (2013) *Urban violence and humanitarian action in Medellín.* Humanitarian Actions in Situations other than War (HASOW). Discussion Paper 5, Available at: http://

DOI: 10.1057/9781137397362.0012

www.cerac.org.co/assets/pdf/Other%20publications/Hasow_6_
Urban%20violence%20and%20humanitarian%20action%20in%20
Medellin_(6jun)_CN.pdf (accessed June 2014).

Betancur, M. S., Stienen, A., & Uran, O. (2001) *Globalización, cadenas productivas & redes de acción colectiva: Reconfiguración territorial y nuevas formas de pobreza y riqueza en Medellín y el Valle de Aburrá.* Santafé de Bogotá: Tercer Mundo Editores.

Betancur, J. J. (2007) Approaches to the regularization of informal settlements: The case of PRIMED in Medellín, Colombia. *Global Urban Development Magazine* 3(1): 1–15.

Blanco, C. & Kobayashi, H. (2009) Urban transformation in slum districts through public space generation and cable transportation at northeastern area: Medellín, Colombia. *Journal of International Social Research* 2(8): 78–90.

Blanco, I., Bonet, J., & Walliser, A. (2011) Urban governance and regeneration policies in historic city centres: Madrid and Barcelona. *Urban research & practice* 4(3): 326–343.

Boudon, L. (1996) Guerrillas and the State: The role of the state in the Colombian peace process. *Journal of Latin American Studies* 28(2): 279–298.

Bourdieu, P. (1991) *Language and symbolic power.* Cambridge, UK: Polity Press.

Brand, P. (2013) Governing inequality in the south through the Barcelona model: 'Social urbanism' in Medellín, Colombia. Conference Paper. 'Interrogating Urban Crisis: Governance, Contestation, Critique', 9–11 September 2013, De Montfort University. Available at: http://www.dmu.ac.uk/documents/business-and-law-documents/research/lgru/peterbrand.pdf (accessed June 2014).

Brand, P., & Dávila, J. D. (2011) Mobility innovation at the urban margins: Medellín's Metrocables. *City* 15(6): 647–661.

Bredenoord, J., & van Lindert, P. (2010) Pro-poor housing policies: Rethinking the potential of assisted self-help housing. *Habitat International* 34(3): 278–287.

Browitt, J. (2001) Capital punishment: The fragmentation of Colombia and the crisis of the nation-state. *Third World Quarterly* 22(6): 1063–1078.

Brush, L. D. (2002) Changing the subject: Gender and welfare regime studies. *Social Politics: International Studies in Gender, State & Society* 9(2): 161–186.

DOI: 10.1057/9781137397362.0012

Burrows, R., Ellison, N., & Woods, B. (2005) *Neighbourhoods on the net: The nature and impact of internet-based neighbourhood information systems.* Bristol, UK: The Policy Press.

Cámara de Comercio (n.d.) *Cluster: Una estrategia para crear ventaja competitiva.* Available at: http://www.camaramedellin.com.co/ site/Biblioteca-virtual/Estudios-economicos/Desarrollo-y-competitividad-regional/Cluster-Estrategia-para-crear-ventaja-competitiva.aspx (accessed June 2013).

Campbell, D., & Dillon, M. (eds) (1993) *The political subject of violence.* Manchester, UK: Manchester University Press.

Carrillo, A. C. (2009) Internal displacement in Colombia: Humanitarian, economic and social consequences in urban settings and current challenges. *International Review of the Red Cross* 91(875): 527–546.

Carroll, L. A. (2011) *Violent democratization: Social movements, elites, and politics in Colombia's rural war zones, 1984–2008.* Notre Dame, IN: University of Notre Dame Press.

Castañeda, J. G. (2003) The forgotten relationship. *Foreign Affairs* 82: 67–81.

Castro, L., & Echeverri, A. (2011) Bogotá and Medellín: Architecture and politics. *Architectural Design* 81(3): 96–103.

Ceballos Melguizo, R., & Cronshaw, F. (2001) The evolution of armed conflict in Medellín: An analysis of the major actors. *Latin American Perspectives* 28(1): 110–131.

Centre for Justice and Accountability (CJA) (n.d.) *Colombia: The justice and peace law.* Available at: http://cja.org/article.php?id=863 (accessed June 2014).

Chant, S. (2002) Researching gender, families and households in Latin America: From the 20th into the 21st century. *Bulletin of Latin American Research* 21(4): 545–575.

Cockburn, C. (2010) Gender relations as causal in militarization and war: A feminist standpoint. *International Feminist Journal of Politics* 12(2): 139–157.

[El] *Colombiano* (2007) *Empresa y academia se unen por un objetivo común.* Available at: http://www.elcolombiano.com/proyectos/ elcolombianoejemplar/premio2007/ganadores/ciencia1.htm (accessed June 2014).

[El] *Colombiano* (2011) *Así nació el Sindicato Antioqueño.* Available at: http://www.elcolombiano.com/BancoConocimiento/A/

DOI: 10.1057/9781137397362.0012

asi_nacio_el_sindicato_antioqueno/asi_nacio_el_sindicato_
antioqueno.asp (accessed June 2014).

[*El*] *Colombiano* (2013) *Arzobispo de Medellín cuestiona situación actual de la ciudad.* Available at http://www.elcolombiano.com/arzobispo_de_medellin_cuestiona_situacion_actual_de_la_ciudad-KEEC_231281 (accessed June 2014).

Concejo de Medellín (2007) *Proyecto 287 de 2006: 'Por medio del cual se modifica el decreto 151 de 2002 y se crea la Secretaría de las Mujeres'.* Available at: http://www.concejodemedellin.gov.co/concejo/concejo/index.php?sub_cat=704#.U5wRiJRdXps (accessed June 2014).

Connell, R. W. (1990) A whole new world: Remaking masculinity in the context of the environmental movement. *Gender & Society* 4(4): 452–478.

Corporación Región (n.d.) *Somos.* Available at: http://www.region.org.co/index.php/somos/mision (accessed June 2014).

Crot, L. (2010) Transnational urban policies: 'Relocating' Spanish and Brazilian models of urban planning in Buenos Aires. *Urban Research & Practice* 3(2): 119–137.

Currid, E., & Williams, S. (2010) The geography of buzz: Art, culture and the social milieu in Los Angeles and New York. *Journal of Economic Geography* 10(3): 423–451.

Dapena Rivera, L. F. (2006) *Núcleos de vida ciudadana: Racionalidades y coyunturas en la gestión de un proyecto urbano.* Universidad Nacional de Colombia. Available at: http://www.bdigital.unal.edu.co/6548/1/tesis03-Dapena.PDF (accessed June 2014).

Dávila, J. D. (2009) Being a mayor: The view from four Colombian cities. *Environment and Urbanization* 21(1): 37–57.

De la Torre, C. (2010) *Populist seduction in Latin America.* Ohio, OH: Ohio University Press.

De Sousa Santos, B. (1998) Participatory budgeting in Porto Alegre: Toward a redistributive democracy. *Politics and Society* 26(4): 461–510.

Devlin, M., & Chaskel, S. (2010) From fear to hope in Colombia: Sergio Fajardo and Medellín, 2004–2007. *Innovations for Successful Societies.* Available at: http://www.princeton.edu/successfulsocieties/policynotes/view.xml?id=116 (accessed June 2014).

DeWall, C. N., Anderson, C. A., & Bushman, B. J. (2011) The general aggression model: Theoretical extensions to violence. *Psychology of Violence* 1(3): 245.

DOI: 10.1057/9781137397362.0012

Diaz, C. (2007) Colombia's bid for justice and peace. In Ambos, K. Large, J., & Wierda, M. (eds) *Building a future on peace and justice.* Berlin, Heidelberg: Springer, 469–501.

Douglas, C. (2008) Barricades and boulevards: Material transformations of Paris, 1795–1871. *Interstice* 8: 31–42.

Drummond, H., Dizgun, J., & Keeling, D. J. (2012) Medellín: A city reborn? *Focus on Geography* 55(4): 146–154.

Echavarría, J. J., Rentería, C., & Steiner, R. (2002) Decentralization and bailouts in Colombia. *Washington DC, Inter-American Development Bank.* Working Papers. Available at: http://idbdocs.iadb.org/wsdocs/getdocument.aspx?docnum=788069 (accessed June 2014).

Echeverri, A., & Orsini, F. (2012) *Informalidad y urbanismo social en Medellín.* Available at: http://upcommons.upc.edu/revistes/bitstream/2099/11900/1/111103_RS3_AEcheverri_%20P%2011-24.pdf (accessed June 2014).

Echeverri, L. M., Rosker, E., & Restrepo, M. L. (2010) Los orígenes de la marca país Colombia es pasión. *Estudios y Perspectivas en Turismo* 19(3): 409–421.

Echeverría Ramírez, M. C., & Bravo Giraldo, M. V. (2009) *Balance sobre el Plan Estratégico de Medellín y el Área Metropolitana.* Medellín Local Government Report. Available at: http://www.medellin.gov.co/irj/go/km/docs/wpccontent/Sites/Subportal%20del%20Ciudadano/Planeaci%C3%B3n%20Municipal/Secciones/Plantillas%20Gen%C3%A9ricas/Documentos/5toCongresoCiudad/Balance%20Plan%20Estrat%C3%A9gico%20de%20Medell%C3%ADn%20y%20el%20%C3%81rea%20Metropolitana.pdf (accessed June 2014).

Ehrenreich, B. (1987) Foreword. In K. Theweleit (ed.) *Male fantasies.* Minneapolis, MN: University of Minnesota Press, ix–xxii.

Elgar, F. J., & Aitken, N. (2011) Income inequality, trust and homicide in 33 countries. *The European Journal of Public Health* 21(2): 241–246.

[El] Espectador (2013) *Ciudades colombianas: Más desiguales.* Available at: http://www.elespectador.com/noticias/nacional/ciudades-colombianas-mas-desiguales-articulo-451323 (accessed June 2014).

Fajardo, A., & Andrews, M. (2014) *Does successful governance require heroes? The case of Sergio Fajardo and the city of Medellín: A reform case for instruction.* WIDER Working Paper. Available at: http://www.wider.unu.edu/publications/working-papers/2014/en_GB/wp2014-035/ (accessed June 2014).

DOI: 10.1057/9781137397362.0012

Fajardo Valderrama, S. (2004) *Medellín: Compromiso de toda la ciudadanía, Plan de Desarrollo 2004–2007.* Alcaldía de Medellín. Available at: http://viva.org.co/cajavirtual/svc0106/articulo11.pdf (accessed June 2014).

Fajardo Valderrama, S. (2007) *Medellín: La más educada.* Alcaldía de Medellín. Available at: http://www.mecd.gob.es/revista-cee/pdf/n6-fajardo-sergio.pdf (accessed June 2014).

Feldman, A. (1991) *Formations of violence: The narrative of the body and political terror in Northern Ireland.* Chicago, IL: University of Chicago Press.

Filippone, R. (1994) The Medellín Cartel: Why we can't win the drug war. *Studies in Conflict & Terrorism* 17(4): 323–344.

Financial Times (2010) *Colombia Turns a New Leaf.* Available at: http://www.ft.com/cms/s/0/ca11fdea-33f1-11e2-9ae7-00144feabdc0.html#ixzz2OUm1EMfD (accessed June 2014).

Flórez, M. (1997) Non-governmental organisations and philanthropy: the Colombian case. *Voluntas: International Journal of Voluntary and Nonprofit Organizations* 8(4): 386–400.

Forbes (2012) *Billionaire druglords: El Chapo Guzman, Pablo Escobar, the Ochoa Brothers.* Available at: http://www.forbes.com/sites/erincarlyle/2012/03/13/billionaire-druglords-el-chapo-guzman-pablo-escobar-the-ochoa-brothers/ (accessed June 2014).

Fouracre, P., Dunkerley, C., & Gardner, G. (2003) Mass rapid transit systems for cities in the developing world. *Transport Reviews* 23(3): 299–310.

Fraser, N. (2004) Hannah Arendt in the 21st century. *Contemporary Political Theory* 3(3): 253–261.

Freeman, J. (2008) Great, good, and divided: The politics of public space in Rio de Janeiro. *Journal of Urban Affairs* 30(5): 529–556.

Fukuyama, F., & Colby, S. (2011) Half a Miracle: Medellín's rebirth is nothing short of astonishing. But have the drug lords really been vanquished? *Foreign Policy.* April 25. Available at: http://www.foreignpolicy.com/articles/2011/04/25/half_a_miracle (accessed June 2014).

Galtung, J. (1969) Violence, peace, and peace research. *Journal of Peace Research* 6(3): 167–191.

Galtung, J. (1990) Cultural violence. *Journal of peace research* 27(3): 291–305.

DOI: 10.1057/9781137397362.0012

García-Herreros, N. F. (2012) Counter-hegemonic constitutionalism: The case of Colombia. *Constellations* 19(2): 235–247.

Gilbert, A. (1997) Employment and poverty during economic restructuring: The case of Bogotá, Colombia. *Urban Studies* 34(7): 1047–1070.

Gilbert, A. (2008) Bus rapid transit: Is Trans Milenio a miracle cure? *Transport Reviews* 28(4): 439–467.

Gill, A. K., Begikhani, N., & Hague, G. (2012) 'Honour'-based violence in Kurdish communities. *Women's Studies International Forum* 35(2) April: 75–85.

Gobernación de Antioquia (2003) *Una paz incluyente y participativa.* Available at http://www.antioquia.gov.co/antioquia-vi/organismos/planeacion/descargas/seguimiento_evalua/evalua_plan_dllo/o3plan_paz.doc (accessed June 2014).

González, S. (2011) Bilbao and Barcelona 'in motion': How urban regeneration 'models' travel and mutate in the global flows of policy tourism. *Urban Studies* 48(7): 1397–1418.

Graham, S. (2011). *Cities under siege: The new military urbanism.* London, UK: Verso.

[The] *Guardian* (2012) *Colombia's architectural tale of two cities.* Available at: http://www.theguardian.com/artanddesign/2012/apr/11/colombia-architecture-bogota-medellin (accessed June 2014).

[The] *Guardian* (2014) *Medellín's metamorphosis provides a beacon for cities across the globe.* Available at: http://www.theguardian.com/business/2014/may/08/medellin-livable-cities-colombia (accessed June 2014).

Gugliotta, G., & Leen, J. (2011) *Kings of cocaine: Inside the Medellín Cartel: an astonishing true story of murder, money and international corruption.* New Orleans, LA: Garrett County Press.

Gutiérrez, F., & Jaramillo A. M. (2004) Crime, (counter-)insurgency and the privatization of security: The case of Medellín, Colombia. *Environment and Urbanization* 16(2): 17–30.

Gutiérrez, F., Pinto, M. T., Arenas, J. C., Guzmán, T., & Gutiérrez, M. T. (2009) *Politics and security in three Colombian cities.* Instituto de Estudios Políticos y Relaciones Internacionales. Available at: http://www.isn.ethz.ch/Digital-Library/Publications/Detail/?ots591=0c54e3b3-1e9c-be1e-2c24-a6a8c7060233&lng=en&id=97580 (accessed June 2014).

DOI: 10.1057/9781137397362.0012

Hall, T., & Robertson, I. (2001) Public art and urban regeneration: Advocacy, claims and critical debates. *Landscape Research* 26(1): 5–26.

Hernandez-García, J. (2013) Slum tourism, city branding and social urbanism: The case of Medellín, Colombia. *Journal of Place Management and Development* 6(1): 43–51.

Herrera, N., & Porch, D. (2008) 'Like going to a fiesta': The role of female fighters in Colombia's FARC-EP. *Small Wars & Insurgencies* 19(4): 609–634.

Human Rights Watch (2011) *Rights out of reach: Obstacles to health, justice, and protection for displaced victims of gender-based violence in Colombia.* Available at: http://www.hrw.org/reports/2012/11/14/rights-out-reach (accessed June 2014).

Hylton, F. (2006) *Evil hour in Colombia.* New York: Verso.

Hylton, F. (2007) Medellín's makeover. *New Left Review* 44: 71–89.

Hylton, F. (2008) *Medellín: The peace of the pacifiers.* NACLA Report on the Americas, 41(1): 35–42.

Inkster, N., & Comolli, V. (2012) The producer states. *Adelphi Series* 52(428): 55–84.

Inroy, N. M. (2000) Urban regeneration and public space: The story of an urban park. *Space and Polity* 4(1): 23–40.

IPC (2013) *Innovemos en seguridad. No hagamos más de lo mismo.* Available at: http://www.ipc.org.co/agenciadeprensa/index. php?option=com_content&view=article&id=704:innovemos-en-seguridad-no-hagamos-mas-de-lo-mismo&catid=37:general&Itemid =150 (accessed June 2014).

IPC (n.d.) *Presentación.* Available at: http://www.ipc.org.co/portal/ (accessed June 2014).

Irazábal, C. (2005) *City making and urban governance in the Americas: Curitiba and Portland.* Aldershot, UK: Ashgate Publishing.

Isaza Castro, J. G. (2003) *Women workers in Bogotá's informal sector: Gendered impact of structural adjustment policies in the 1990s.* Departamento Nacional de Planeación. Available at: http:// econpapers.repec.org/paper/col000118/003784.htm (accessed June 2014).

Issacson, A. (2014) *Ending 50 years of conflict: The challenges ahead and the U.S. role in Colombia.* Washington Office on Latin America. Available at: http://colombiapeace.org/files/1404_colpeace.pdf (accessed June 2014).

DOI: 10.1057/9781137397362.0012

Jabri, V. (1996) *Discourses on violence: Conflict analysis reconsidered.* Manchester, UK: Manchester University Press.

Jones, G. A., & Rodgers, D. (eds) (2009) *Youth violence in Latin America.* New York: Palgrave Macmillan.

Jones, G. A., & Rodgers, D. (2011) The World Bank's World Development Report 2011 on conflict, security and development: A critique through five vignettes. *Journal of International Development* 23(7): 980–995.

Kavaratzis, M. (2004) From city marketing to city branding: Towards a theoretical framework for developing city brands. *Place branding* 1(1): 58–73.

Koch, Julie (2006) Collectivism or isolation? Gender relations in urban La Paz, Bolivia. *Bulletin of Latin American Research* 25(1): 43–62.

Kronsell, A., & Svedberg, E. (eds) (2011) *Making gender, making war: Violence, military and peacekeeping practices.* New York: Routledge.

Kurtz, M. J. (2004) The dilemmas of democracy in the open economy: Lessons from Latin America. *World Politics* 56(2): 262–302.

Lamb, D. (2010) *Microdynamics of illegitimacy and complex urban violence in Medellín, Colombia.* Unpublished Doctoral Thesis, University of Maryland. Available at http://drum.lib.umd.edu/handle/1903/10242 (accessed June 2014).

Larner, W., & Laurie, N. (2010) Travelling technocrats, embodied knowledges: Globalising privatisation in telecoms and water. *Geoforum* 41(2): 218–226.

LaRosa, M. J., & Mejía, G. R. (2012) *Colombia: A concise contemporary history.* Plymouth, UK: Rowman & Littlefield.

Lee, R. W. (1991) *The white labyrinth: Cocaine and political power.* New Brunswick, NJ: Transaction Publishers.

Lees, L. (1998) Urban renaissance and the street: Spaces of control and contestation. In N. Fyfe (ed.) *Images of the street: planning, identity and control in public space.* New York: Routledge.

Lees, L. (2012) The geography of gentrification: Thinking through comparative urbanism. *Progress in Human Geography* 36(2): 155–171.

Lees, L., Slater, T., & Wyly, E. (2010) *The gentrification reader.* London: Routledge

Lind, W. S. (2004) Understanding fourth generation war. *Military Review* 84(5): 12–16.

Lindau, L. A., Hidalgo, D., & Facchini, D. (2010) Curitiba, the cradle of bus rapid transit. *Built Environment* 36(3): 274–282.

DOI: 10.1057/9781137397362.0012

Lopez, M. & Kuc, M. (2009) Medellín: El Hueco as a public space. *Gestion y Ambiente* 12(1): 130–147.

Lowenthal, A. F., & Rojas Mejía, P. (2010) Medellín: Front line of Colombia's challenges. *Americas Quarterly* Winter: 148–152.

McCann, E. (2002) Space, citizenship, and the right to the city: A brief overview. *GeoJournal* 58(2): 77–79.

McCann, E., & Ward, K. (eds) (2011) *Mobile urbanism: Cities and policymaking in the global age.* Minneapolis, MN: University of Minnesota Press.

Maclean, K. (2013) Risk, responsibility and gendered microfinancial subjectivities. *Antipode* 45(2): 455–473.

Maclean, K. (2014a) *The Medellín Miracle: The politics of elites, crises and coalitions.* Developmental Leadership Program. Available at: http://www.dlprog.org/publications/executive-summary-the-medellin-miracle.php (accessed June 2014).

Maclean, K. (2014b) Evo's jumper: Identity and the used clothes trade in 'post-neoliberal', 'pluri-cultural' Bolivia. *Gender, Place & Culture* 21(8): 963–978.

Maclean, K. (2015) Gender, risk and the Wall Street alpha male. *Journal of Gender Studies.* Early view available at: http://dx.doi.org/10.1080/09589236.2014.990425.

MacLeod, G. (2002) From urban entrepreneurialism to a 'revanchist city'? On the spatial injustices of Glasgow's renaissance. *Antipode* 34(3): 602–624.

Mazur, A. (2013) Dominance, violence, and the neurohormonal nexus. In Frank, T. & Turner, J. (eds) *Handbook of neurosociology.* Netherlands: Springer, 359–368.

Medellín Ciudad Cluster (n.d.) *Qué es Medellín Ciudad Cluster?* Available at: http://www.Medellínciudadcluster.com/ (accessed June 2014).

Moncada, E. (2013) The politics of urban violence: Challenges for development in the global south. *Studies in Comparative International Development* 48(3): 217–239.

Monclús, F. J. (2003) The Barcelona model: And an original formula? From 'reconstruction' to strategic urban projects (1979–2004). *Planning perspectives* 18(4): 399–421.

Monitor (1994) *Creando la ventaja competitiva de Colombia.* Available at http://camara.ccb.org.co/contenido/contenido.aspx?catID=83&conID=1267 (accessed June 2014).

DOI: 10.1057/9781137397362.0012

Moser, C. O. (2004) Urban violence and insecurity: An introductory roadmap. *Environment and Urbanisation* 16(2): 3–16.

Moser, C. O., & McIlwaine, C. (2004) *Encounters with violence in Latin America.* London: Routledge.

Moser, C. O., & McIlwaine, C. (2006) Latin American urban violence as a development concern: Towards a framework for violence reduction. *World Development* 34(1): 89–112.

Muggah, R. (ed.) (2013) *Stabilization operations, security and development: States of fragility.* London: Routledge.

Muggah, R., & Savage, K. (2012) Urban violence and humanitarian action: Engaging the fragile city. *The Journal of Humanitarian Assistance.* Available at: http://sites.tufts.edu/jha/archives/1524 (accessed June 2014).

Munck, R. (2008) Introduction: Deconstructing violence: Power, force, and social transformation. *Latin American Perspectives* 35(5): 3–19.

Murdock, D. F. (2008) *When women have wings: Feminism and development in Medellín, Colombia.* Ann Arbor, MI: University of Michigan Press.

NACLA (2009) *Legalizing the illegal: Paramilitarism in Colombia's 'post-paramilitary' era.* Available at: https://nacla.org/files/A04204014_1.pdf (accessed June 2014).

Newman, O. (1973) *Defensible space: Crime prevention through urban design.* New York: Collier Books.

New York Times (1999) *Medellín Journal: A terrorized university fights to be true to itself.* Available at: http://www.nytimes.com/1999/12/28/world/Medellín-journal-a-terrorized-university-fights-to-be-true-to-itself.html (accessed June 2014).

New York Times (2004) *Surge in extradition of Colombia drug suspects to U.S.* Available at: http://www.nytimes.com/2004/12/06/international/americas/06colombia.html?pagewanted=print&position=&_r=0 (accessed June 2014).

New York Times (2012) *A city rises along with its hopes.* Available at: http://www.nytimes.com/2012/05/20/arts/design/fighting-crime-with-architecture-in-medellin-colombia.html?_r=0 (accessed June 2014).

Nordstrom, C., & Robben, A. C. (eds) (1995) *Fieldwork under fire: Contemporary studies of violence and survival.* Berkeley, Los Angeles, & London: University of California Press.

Novy, A., & Leubolt, B. (2005) Participatory budgeting in Porto Alegre: Social innovation and the dialectical relationship of state and civil society. *Urban Studies* 42(11): 2023–2036.

DOI: 10.1057/9781137397362.0012

OECD (2012) *Higher education in regional and city development.* Paris, France: OECD Publishing.

O'Reilly, M. (2012) Muscular interventionism: Gender, power and liberal peacebuilding in post-conflict Bosnia-Herzegovina. *International Feminist Journal of Politics* 14(4): 529–548.

Palacios, M. (2006) *Between legitimacy and violence: A history of Colombia, 1875–2002.* Durham, NC: Duke University Press.

Pearce, J. (2006) Bringing violence 'back home': Gender socialisation and the transmission of violence through time and space. In Albrow, M., Anheier, H. K., Glasius, M., Price, M. E., & Kaldor, M. (eds) *Global civil society 2007/8: Communicative power and democracy.* London, UK: Sage, 42–61.

Pécaut, D. (1999) From the banality of violence to real terror: The case of Colombia. In Koonings, K., & Krujit, D. (eds) *Societies of fear: The legacy of civil war, violence and terror in Latin America.* London, UK: Zed Books, 141–167.

Peck, J., & Theodore, N. (2010) Mobilizing policy: Models, methods, and mutations. *Geoforum* 41(2): 169–174.

Personería de Medellín (2011). *Informe sobre la situación de Derechos Humanos en Medellín.* Available at: http://www.personeriamedellin. gov.co/documentos/documentos/Informes/Situacion_DDHH2011/ Informe-ddhh-2011-1.pdf (accessed October 2014).

Petras, J. (2000) Geopolitics of Plan Colombia. *Economic and Political Weekly*, 4617–4623.

Pratt, A. C. (2011) The cultural contradictions of the creative city. *City, Culture and Society* 2(3): 123–130.

Pridemore, W. A. (2011). Poverty matters: A reassessment of the inequality – homicide relationship in cross-national studies. *British Journal of Criminology* 51(5): 739–772.

Pro-Antioquia (n.d.) *Qiuenes Somos.* Available at: http://proantioquia. org.co/web/index.php/quienes-somos-aspectos-generales (accessed June 2014).

Purcell, M. (2002) Excavating Lefebvre: The right to the city and its urban politics of the inhabitant. *GeoJournal* 58(2–3): 99–108.

Raco, M. (2013) *State-led privatisation and the demise of the democratic state: Welfare reform and localism in an era of regulatory capitalism.* London, UK: Ashgate Publishing.

Restrepo Santamaria, N. (2011) *Empresariado antioqueño y sociedad, 1940–2004: Influencia de las elites patronales de Antioquia en las*

DOI: 10.1057/9781137397362.0012

políticas socioeconómicas colombianas. Medellín, Colombia: Editorial Universidad de Antioquia.

Riley, E., Fiori, J., & Ramírez, R. (2001) Favela Bairro and a new generation of housing programmes for the urban poor. *Geoforum* 32(4): 521–531.

Robinson, J. (2006) *Ordinary cities: Between modernity and development.* London: Routledge.

Rocha, R. (2011) *The new dimensions of narco-trafficking in Colombia.* Oficina de las Naciones Unidas contra la Droga y el Delito. Available at: http://www.mamacoca.org/docs_de_base/Cifras_cuadro_mamacoca/RochaRicardo_Las_Nuevas_Dimensiones_del_Narcotrafic_2011.pdf (accessed June 2014).

Rodgers, D. & Muggah, R. (2009) Gangs as non-state armed groups: The Central American case. *Contemporary Security Policy* 30(2): 301–317.

Rojas, C., Anderlini, S. N., & Conaway, C. P. (2004) *In the midst of war: Women's contributions to peace in Colombia.* Women Waging Peace Policy Commission, Hunt Alternatives Fund. Available at: http://www.inclusivesecurity.org/wp-content/uploads/2012/08/16_in_the_midst_of_war_women_s_contributions_to_peace_in_colombia.pdf (accessed June 2014).

Roldán, M. (1997) Citizenship, class and violence in historical perspective: The Colombian case. Conference Paper. Annual Meeting of Latin American Studies Association, Guadalajara, Mexico April 17–19. Available at: http://bibliotecavirtual.clacso.org.ar/ar/libros/lasa97/roldan.pdf (accessed June 2014).

Roldán, M. (1999) Colombia: Cocaine and the 'Miracle' of modernity in Medellín. In p. Gootenberg (ed.) *Cocaine: Global histories.* New York: Routledge, 165–182.

Roldán, M. (2002) *Blood and fire: La Violencia in Antioquia, Colombia, 1946–1953.* Chapel Hill, NC: Duke University Press.

Rozema, R. (2008) Urban DDR-processes: Paramilitaries and criminal networks in Medellín, Colombia. *Journal of Latin American Studies* 40(3): 423–452.

Samper, J. (2012) The role of urban upgrading in Latin America as warfare tool against the 'slums wars'. *Critical Planning* Summer: 58–76.

Sato, M. (2013) *A fresh look at capacity development from insiders' perspectives: A case study of an urban redevelopment project in Medellín, Colombia.* JICA Working Paper 60. Available at: http://repository.ri.jica.go.jp/dspace/bitstream/10685/94/1/JICA-RI_WP_No.60_2013_2.pdf (accessed June 2014).

DOI: 10.1057/9781137397362.0012

Schwab, E. (2013) New public open spaces and old prejudices: Public space uses in the centre of Medellín. *Real Corp Planning Times*, 627–637. Available at: http://www.corp.at/archive/CORP2013_123.pdf (accessed June 2014).

Semana (1990) *El cuarto de hora de Antioquia*. Available at: http://www.semana.com/nacion/articulo/el-cuarto-de-hora-de-antioquia/13908-3 (accessed June 2014).

Semana (1993) *Se va 'La monita'*. Available at: http://www.semana.com/gente/articulo/se-va-la-monita/19295-3 (accessed June 2014).

Sen, A. (2007) *Identity and violence: The illusion of destiny*. London, UK: Penguin Books.

Sennett, R. (1977) *The fall of public man*. New York: Alfred A. Knopf.

Sharp, J., Pollock, V., & Paddison, R. (2005) Just art for a just city: Public art and social inclusion in urban regeneration. *Urban Studies* 42(5–6): 1001–1023.

Simone, A. (2002) The dilemmas of informality. In Parnell, S.. Pieterse, E., Swilling, M., & Wooldridge, D. (eds) *Democratising local government: The South African experiment*. Cape Town, South Africa: University of Cape Town Press, 204–219.

Skaperdas, S. (2001) The political economy of organized crime: Providing protection when the State does not. *Economics of Governance* 2(3): 173–202.

Sklair, L. (2010) Iconic architecture and the culture-ideology of consumerism. *Theory, Culture & Society* 27(5): 135–159.

Slater, T. (2004) North American gentrification? Revanchist and emancipatory perspectives explored. *Environment and Planning A* 36(7): 1191–1214.

Slater, T. (2010). Revanchist city. In R. Hutchison (ed.) *Encyclopedia of urban studies*. Thousand Oaks, CA: Sage, 666–668.

Smith, J. E. (2014) *Cocaine cowgirl: The outrageous life and mysterious death of Griselda Blanco, the godmother of Medellín*. San Francisco, CA: Byliner Inc.

Smith, N. (2002) New globalism, new urbanism: Gentrification as global urban strategy. *Antipode* 34(3): 427–450.

Smith, N. (2012) *The new urban frontier: Gentrification and the revanchist city*. New York: Routledge.

Smith, W. C., Acuña, C. H., & Gamarra, E. A. (eds) (1994) *Latin American political economy in the age of neoliberal reform: Theoretical and comparative perspectives for the 1990s*. New Brunswick, NJ: Transaction Publishers.

DOI: 10.1057/9781137397362.0012

Spagnolo, L., & Munevar, D. (2008) *After years of (economic) solitude: Neoliberal reforms and pay inequality in Colombia.* The University of Texas Inequality Project Working Paper. Available at: http://utip. gov.utexas.edu/papers/utip_47.pdf (accessed June 2014).

Stienen, A. (2009) Urban technology, conflict education, and disputed space. *Journal of Urban Technology* 16(2–3): 109–142.

Stokes, D. (2001) Better lead than bread? A critical analysis of the US's Plan Colombia. *Civil Wars* 4(2): 59–78.

Taussig, M. (1984) Culture of terror – space of death: Roger Casement's Putumayo report and the explanation of torture. *Comparative Studies in Society and History* 26(3): 467–497.

Taussig, M. (2005) *Law in a lawless land: Diary of a limpieza in Colombia.* Chicago, IL: University of Chicago Press.

[El] *Tiempo* (1991) *Medellín pide apoyo a CEE.* Available at: http://www. eltiempo.com/archivo/documento/MAM-191279 (accessed June 2014).

[El] *Tiempo* (1992) *Medellín: Alternativas de futuro.* Available at: http:// www.eltiempo.com/archivo/documento/MAM-111136 (accessed June 2014).

Tilly, C. (2003) *The politics of collective violence.* Cambridge, UK: Cambridge University Press.

Tizro, Z. (2013) *Domestic violence in Iran: Women, marriage and Islam.* New York: Routledge.

Tubb, D. (2013) Narratives of citizenship in Medellín, Colombia. *Citizenship Studies* 17(5): 627–640.

UNDP (2013) *Citizen security with a human face: Evidence and proposals for Latin America.* Available at: http://www.undp.org/content/undp/ en/home/librarypage/hdr/human-development-report-for-latin-america-2013-2014.html (accessed December 2014)

UN Human Settlements Programme (2007) *Enhancing urban safety and security: Global report on human settlements 2007.* Available at: http:// mirror.unhabitat.org/pmss/listItemDetails.aspx?publicationID=2432 (accessed June 2014).

Uran, O. (2010) Medellín: Participatory creativity in a conflictive city. In J. Pearce (ed.) *Participation and democracy in the 21st century city.* New York: Palgrave Macmillan, 127–153.

Vaicius, I., & Isacson, A. (2003) The 'war on drugs' meets the 'war on terror'. *International Policy Report* 2(6): 1–27.

DOI: 10.1057/9781137397362.0012

Valencia Agudelo, G. D., Pulgarín, M. L. A., & Acosta, J. H. F. (2009) Capital social, desarrollo y políticas públicas en Medellín, 2004–2007. *Estudios Políticos* 32: 53–83.

Valenzuela Delgado, L. C. (1999) Dónde están las élites? El problema de Colombia. *Estudios Gerenciales* 72: 33–35.

Varela Barrios, Edgar (2011) *Políticas y estrategias en la gestión de EPM Medellín.* Colombia: Ediciones de la U.

Villar, L., & Rincón, H. (2000) *The Colombian economy in the nineties: Capital flows and foreign exchange regimes.* Banco de la República, Subgerencia de Estudios Económica. Available at: http://www.banrep.gov.co/docum/ftp/borra149.pdf (accessed October 2014).

Wacquant, L. (2009) *Punishing the poor: The neoliberal government of social insecurity.* Durham, NC: Duke University Press.

Wall Street Journal (2013) *City of the year.* Available at: http://online.wsj.com/ad/cityoftheyear (accessed June 2014).

Ward, K. (2006) 'Policies in motion', urban management and state restructuring: The trans-local expansion of business improvement districts. *International Journal of Urban and Regional Research* 30(1): 54–75.

Ward, K. (2011) Entrepreneurial urbanism, policy tourism, and the making mobile of policies. In Bridge, G. & Watson, S. (eds) *The new companion to the city.* Oxford, UK: Wiley-Blackwell.

[*The*] *Washington Post* (2010) Medellín, Colombia: From drugs violence to tourist destination. Available at: http://www.washingtonpost.com/wp-dyn/content/article/2010/11/19/AR2010111902827.html (accessed June 2014).

Watson, V. (2009) Seeing from the South: Refocusing urban planning on the globe's central urban issues. *Urban Studies* 46(11): 2259–2275.

Weizman, E. (2012) *Hollow land: Israel's architecture of occupation.* New York: Verso.

Weyland, K. (2004) Neoliberalism and democracy in Latin America: A mixed record. *Latin American Politics and Society*, 46(1): 135–157.

World Health Organisation (WHO) (2014) *Definition and typology of violence.* Available at: http://www.who.int/violenceprevention/approach/definition/en/ (accessed June 2014).

Winton, A. (2004) Urban violence: A guide to the literature. *Environment and Urbanization* 16(2): 165–184.

World Bank (2010) Violence in the city: Understanding and supporting community responses to urban violence. Available at: http://

DOI: 10.1057/9781137397362.0012

siteresources.worldbank.org/EXTSOCIALDEVELOPMENT/
Resources/244362-1164107274725/Violence_in_the_City.pdf (accessed
June 2014).

Wright, M. W. (2004) From protests to politics: Sex work, women's
worth, and Ciudad Juárez modernity. *Annals of the Association of
American Geographers* 94(2): 369–386.

DOI: 10.1057/9781137397362.0012

Index

DOI: 10.1057/9781137397362.0013

Ejército de Liberación Nacional
 [ELN], 34, 43, 81
Fuerzas Armadas Revolucionarias
 de Colombia [FARC], 4, 5, 30,
 31, 34, 43, 44, 45, 47, 48, 79, 81,
 82, 85, 104, 105, 107
Milicia del Pueblo, 43
Movimiento 19 de Abril [M19], 34,
 43
Urban militia, 2, 5, 30–34, 43–47, 51,
 67, 96
Liberation Theology, 104–106, 110
Libraries, 7, 51, 55, 63, 64, 66–68, 93,
 122, 124
London, 23, 58, 66

Mao Zedong, 15
Masculinity, 14, 18, 21, 48, 50, 51, 114,
 118
Medellín:
 Chamber of Commerce, 73, 75, 91,
 92
 Comunas, 30, 32–35, 38, 41, 42, 46, 51,
 59, 68, 71, 73, 74, 102, 108, 109,
 111, 122, 124
 Country Club, 36
 Development Plans, 63, 111, 113
 Industrialisation, 35, 109
 Industry, 35, 36, 37, 73, 94
 Invisible borders, 33
 Marginalised areas, 3, 5, 20, 27, 55, 57,
 58, 65, 93, 119
 Poblado, El, 4, 32, 36, 41, 55, 87, 93
 Rapid growth, 8, 30, 31, 33
 San Javier, 32, 47, 61
 Santo Domingo, 32, 61
Mejía, Maria Emma, 88, 118
Metro, 55, 60, 61
Metrocable, 7, 47, 51, 55, 58, 60, 61, 90,
 93, 124
Mexico, 19, 39, 54, 58
Migration, 4, 21, 22, 30–32, 37, 57, 66
Military, 3, 11, 16, 17, 18, 23, 24, 31, 34,
 43–48, 76, 80–84, 88, 89
Model cities, 54, 56–59, 61–63,
 69, 75

Modernisation, 20, 22, 25, 26, 59, 92,
 102, 104, 114, 116
Monitor Group, 79, 88, 91, 95, 101, 109

Naranjo, Sergio, 93
Narco-traffic, 21–23, 31, 32, 33, 36–38,
 41, 42, 44, 45, 48, 50, 51, 54, 79,
 80, 81, 91, 95, 102, 123
Non-governmental organisations
 [NGOs], 8, 33, 68, 74, 80, 85, 88,
 89, 96, 99, 100–106, 109, 124

Operación Mariscal, 47, 82
Operación Orión, 47, 82
Opus Dei, 105

Pacification, 3, 23, 47, 82
Paramilitarism, 2, 3, 4, 5, 17, 20, 30–34,
 38, 39, 42–48, 51, 67, 72, 79,
 81–83, 96, 103, 120, 124
Paramilitary groups:
 Autodefensas Unidas de Colombia
 [AUC], 82
 Bloque Cacique Nutibara [BCN], 83
 Las Convivir, 46, 47
 Perseguidos por Pablo Escobar
 [PePEs], 44, 45
Paramilitary leaders:
 Carlos Castaño, 45, 103
 Don Berna, 82
Paris, 25, 56
Parks, 7, 55, 63–68, 71, 73, 93, 122
Participation, 6, 25, 26, 35, 55, 62–64,
 67, 69–76, 79, 85, 86, 89, 94, 96,
 101, 105, 106, 109, 111–118, 123
Participatory budget, 25, 71, 72, 109,
 112, 113
Pastrana Arango, Andrés, 80, 81
Patronage, 35–38, 41, 43, 63
Peace, 13, 19, 43, 45, 46, 81, 82, 83, 105,
 106, 107, 117, 118
Plan Colombia, 80–82
Plan Estrátegio para Medellín, 90, 99,
 100
Plan Lazo, 34
Police, 20, 40, 41, 45, 46, 88

DOI: 10.1057/9781137397362.0013

DOI: 10.1057/9781137397362.0013

DOI: 10.1057/9781137397362.0013

Lightning Source UK Ltd.
Milton Keynes UK
UKOW04n0701230215

246695UK00004B/7/P